W9-BGP-447

METS ESSENTIAL

Everything You Need to Know
to Be a Real Fan!

Matthew Silverman

TRIUMPH
BOOKS

Library of Congress Cataloging-in-Publication Data

Silverman, Matthew, 1965–
    Mets essential : everything you need to know to be a real fan! / Matthew Silverman.
        p. cm.
    Includes bibliographical references.
    ISBN: 978-1-57243-848-4
        1. New York Mets (Baseball team) I. Title.

GV875.N45S55 2007
796.357'64097471—dc22

                                                                2006067637

This book is available in quantity at special discounts for your group or organization. For further information, contact:

Triumph Books
542 South Dearborn Street
Suite 750
Chicago, Illinois 60605
(312) 939-3330
Fax (312) 663-3557

Printed in U.S.A.
ISBN: 978-1-57243-848-4
Design by Patricia Frey
All photos courtesy of AP/Wide World Photos except where otherwise indicated

To Linc Wonham

My double-play partner in high school, he's an even better person than he is a ballplayer. Before we attended dozens of games together, I remember going down the wrong row and coming across him accidentally in a rarely packed Shea Stadium upper deck in 1980. You always run into the best people at Shea.

Contents

Foreword

This is the story of a baseball club.

The word *story* is purposely used in lieu of the common designation of *history*. A baseball club rarely has a history in the strictest sense of the word. The record of its formation and growth more closely resembles, instead, a biography. A baseball club, perhaps more than any other entity, assumes a human personality, because each club mirrors a character all its own.

For me, that character has been revealed through four different dimensions—the players, the staff, my broadcast colleagues, and the city it represents.

I have been honored to be a part of the New York Mets family as an announcer and color commentator ever since the team's initial year on this planet—1962. During this time, from the unique standpoint that pioneer broadcaster Red Barber called "the catbird seat," I have seen, firsthand, the story of the New York Mets as shown by all four phases of its character.

The players formed a cast of dynamic personalities that would be the envy of any best-selling novelist.

I knew, both as a player and a manager, Gil Hodges, a class act who personified the title "gentleman." This quiet, gentle giant could have been a role model for Mother Teresa.

I saw Darryl Strawberry and Dwight Gooden—two players with outstanding credentials—who, in my opinion, during their rookie seasons were shoo-ins for the Hall of Fame. Today, I wonder what they could have become had they not allowed personal problems to overwhelm them.

On a more positive side, I watched fireballing Tom Seaver mature from a raw rookie just out of the University of Southern California into one of the most consistent pitchers in baseball history, en route to winning three Cy Young Awards.

Was there ever a more effective rallying cry than "Ya Gotta Believe!" authored by ace reliever Tug McGraw?

In spite of the team's miserable first seasons, players such as "Marvelous" Marv Throneberry, Ed Kranepool, and Richie Ashburn endeared the Mets to their hometown fans.

From the dugout, certain managers added even more color to the scene. As a result, Casey Stengel, Joe Torre, Davey Johnson, Yogi Berra, and Willie Randolph became sources coveted by reporters for quotes about the games.

I shed a tear when catcher Mike Piazza, at the first home game following the disaster of 9/11, handed the first-pitched baseball to the home-plate umpire, who, in turn, took it over to Mayor Rudolph Giuliani to the heartfelt cheers of a packed Shea Stadium.

Most appealing to me, as well as to the rest of the fans, were players who gave every ounce of energy to the game. Lenny Dykstra, Gary Carter, and Mookie Wilson, for example, were throwbacks to the "dirty-shirt ballplayers" of the old Gashouse Gang in St. Louis.

With mixed emotions, I saw some legends of the game—Willie Mays and Warren Spahn—struggle against the inevitable consequences of age as they attempted to add one more season to their careers in Major League Baseball.

I have renewed optimism for the club whenever I see young stars, such as David Wright and Jose Reyes, entering their prime.

Guiding the Mets with their knowledge of the game and with their pocketbooks were some benevolent owners, such as Joan Payson, Fred Wilpon, and Nelson Doubleday, as well as general managers, including George Weiss, Frank Cashen, and Omar Minaya.

My broadcast colleagues, all of whom I have learned from over the years, left their marks on the game and on me. These lifelong friends include Lindsey Nelson, Tim McCarver, Bob Murphy (who was as close to a brother as I'll ever have), Steve Zabriskie, Rusty Staub, Gary Thorne, Art Shamsky, Keith Hernandez, Ron Darling, Gary Cohen, and Fran Healy.

Finally, I feel deeply honored to have met so many of you fans who have crossed through the turnstiles at Shea Stadium. I can say, without reservation, that New York fans are the most knowledgeable about the game. Perhaps this is one of the reasons why Mets fans react strongly to a player who may not have hustled down the first-base line, and why they support with uncanny loyalty those who give 100 percent on each play.

The tales and statistics you'll read in this book will reveal much about the New York Mets. That said, the best way for you or anyone else to learn about the team is to join us at Shea Stadium and see a new chapter in the team's history unfold before your very eyes.

—Ralph Kiner

Acknowledgments

Many have come before me, and more will follow. There are numerous sources on the Mets, from books to websites. Several sources listed in the Notes section were vital to this endeavor. The books below were helpful in bringing fact to memory and helping new ideas take shape: Daily News *Scrapbook History of the New York Mets 1986 Season* (New York News Inc., 1987); *The Team by Team Encyclopedia of Major League Baseball* (Purdy, Dennis. New York: Workman Publishing, 2006); *Total Baseball.* (Thorn, John, Palmer, Pete, et al. Kingston, New York: Total Sports Publishing, 2001); and *Total Mets* (Thorn, John, Palmer, Pete, et al. Total Sports, 1997).

All statistics were taken from *The 2006 ESPN Baseball Encyclopedia* (New York: Sterling Publishing, 2006). Kudos to my other favorite team: Gary Gillette, Pete Palmer, Stu Shea, Doug White, Greg Spira, and Sean Lahman. There are many valuable baseball websites, but the ones I looked to most for general baseball info were retrosheet.com and baseball-reference.com. Baseball-almanac.com also provides plenty of food for thought. Mets morale builders in cyberspace are always available at Faith and Fear in Flushing (fearandfaith.blogharbor.com), Ultimate Mets Database (ultimatemets.com), and Mets by the Numbers (mbtn.net). Extra credit goes to Bruce Markusen and Robert Pizzella, who were there with me during the Grant's Tomb era and reconnected years later. Also thanks to Jon Springer, Paul Lovetere, and Alec Dawson.

The websites, books, and media guides were tremendous resources, but perhaps the most surprising source was a trove of 1960s and 1970s Mets yearbooks dug out of Brad Smith's attic and given to me because he knew I'd never throw them away. The details by the Mets PR team in player bios—plus minor league records—were inspirational, insightful, and made this project more enjoyable. Latter-day media guides and programs were likewise a gold mine.

Triumph Books had the foresight to commission this book to coincide with the most thrilling Mets season in years. Thanks to Jessica Paumier for her patience and skill during the final stages, which coincided with a hectic postseason.

Books like this aren't possible without family support. My Aunt Virginia always had her radio tuned to Lindsey Nelson's mellifluous voice. My father, Syd, constantly neglected his off-day pursuits to take me to Shea at my whim, which was often. Many years ago my mother, Jan, secretly and neatly packed away so many of the things I would need for this project; her foresight and caring lives on. Mike Gershman hired me and set me to work on my first Mets book a decade ago. My wife, Debbie, did not have to convert religions, but she willingly switched denominations from Fenway to Shea. Our children, Jan and Tyler, came out knowing Wright from Evil.

And for anyone who saw the likes of Pepe Mangual, Roy Staiger, and Dyar Miller, and lived to tell the tale, I wrote every sentence with you in mind.

Introduction

Mets fans are among the greatest fans in the world. I can't say *the* greatest because there are fans of other teams with much less success who have cheered their clubs on without complaint, and Mets fans have been known not to hold in their displeasure. New York is a tough town. It's also a great place for baseball. The first postseason game at Shea Stadium in six years crackled with excitement; fans roared on every pitch. Kids who were in diapers for the club's last postseason appearance were indoctrinated in 2006. Older fans who'd stayed the course were validated. Shea shook once more. This was the payoff for all that hard work, for all that patience.

Mets fans get credit because they hold their own in a city, in a state, in a world, that is coursing with Yankees fans. Yankees fans are as thick as weeds hundreds of miles from the Bronx and yet there is always a patch of Mets fans trying to grow toward the light. Logic says you should root for the Yankees, but you can't, you won't, you'd sooner follow badminton. Baseball isn't about logic. Casey Stengel took care of that as the club's first manager.

Part of the National League's first expansion in 70 years, the Mets replaced New York's two sacred trusts: the Brooklyn Dodgers and the New York Giants. Whereas those teams ran to California, the Mets put down roots in 1962 and promised to stay. Fans promised to love them, no matter what. They laughed through 120 losses and begged for more. Casey and the papers called them "the new breed."

This breed showed its love from the beginning by writing its feelings on sheets because it would be hard to read if they just wore them on their sleeves. "Placards," Casey called the signs. The Mets turned this Polo Grounds tradition into Banner Day, when fans were allowed onto the field with their signs between games of a double-header. That tradition lasted through Marvelous Marv, Rocky Swoboda, and the Glider, through Kooz, Kong, and Tom Terrific, through Lenny, Mookie, and Mex. It outlasted the doubleheader itself, until Banner Day finally petered out a decade ago. But it's taken on a new voice in the technology age as fans express their thoughts and feelings for the club on websites, blogs, and message boards. Mets fans in Phoenix can watch, listen, or read along with every pitch from New York on their computers.

Or they can still go to Shea, baseball's most maligned park, slated for replacement by Citi Field for the 2009 season. No modern-day Sign Man can match Karl Ehrhardt, who had a sign for every occasion from the field box seats, and no canned music will ever supplant memories of Jane Jarvis's organ, but the new breed keeps alive the tradition and the spirit. Cow Bell Man, Meet the Matts, orange fedoras, Reyes wigs, and all those people with blue and orange face paint would make Casey proud.

Three million plus streamed into Shea in 2006 despite high prices and tough parking. It's no grand palace of baseball, for sure, but no new-age park can rekindle the magical moments or nostalgia of Shea: the black cat, the shoe-polish incident, the carom that ate Richie Zisk, Dykstra's dinger, the slow roller, Pratt's blast, the grand-slam single, and Lo Duca's double tag at the plate. Fans will wince on that first strike of the wrecker's ball.

"You Gotta Have Heart." That's what Mets players joyously sang after their 1969 World Series slaying of the Baltimore Orioles (ironically, that was the franchise name the New York Yankees began their existence under before coming north in 1903). That song came from *Damn Yankees*, a musical about a man selling his soul to beat the Yankees. While that show was written about the Washington Senators before the Mets were a gleam in William Shea or Branch Rickey's eye, it might as well have been about the Mets. Since the start of interleague play in 1997, some Mets fans have become singly obsessed with beating the Yankees or wishing them ill. Indeed, derogatory Yankees chants can break out any time at Shea Stadium, even against the Pirates. Maybe it's because they all know how close they could have been to being Yankees fans. While many Mets fans are born into Mets households, many find their way to Shea by different means.

However they get there, they embrace a rich tale that's truly American. Not everyone can be a monolithic entity; most people can't aspire to that or ever hope of getting there. But with a little spit and polish, and some wheeling and dealing from Johnny, Frank, or Omar, maybe this is the year. If not this year, next. Mets fans don't consider a season a failure if they don't win the championship; every year, every day, builds toward a better tomorrow. Cherish the past, enjoy the present, look to the future. And let's go, Mets!

The Mahatma and the Conjuring of the Mets

Among the many achievements in the career of the great Branch Rickey, his role in the creation of the New York Mets is pretty far down the list. After all, his signing of Jackie Robinson and establishing the model for the farm system were two revolutionary concepts that faced major opposition. He also built the first Cardinals world championship club in 1926 after the franchise had endured 35 seasons of terrible play, he started the 1950s Pirates back from similar depths, he changed the way teams approached spring training, and he stuck around the major leagues as a marginal player long enough to get his foot in the front office door. So what did the Mahatma have to do with the founding of the Mets? In six decades of major league baseball, Rickey knew one thing that got the attention of the men in the ivory tower of the owner's box: competition for the public's dollars.

New York was smarting badly after the loss of two clubs to the West Coast after the 1957 season. Before the 1950s, the last major league franchise to relocate was a team that moved *to* New York: the Yankees. Yes, the Yankees, the representative of all things New York, came to the city as just another transplant. The team moved from Baltimore in 1903, after John McGraw and others conspired to bleed the original American League Orioles dry of talent and then jump on the real baseball opportunity in New York at the time: the Giants. The 1904 World Series was not played partly because McGraw and Giants owner John Brush feared that the transplanted club, the Highlanders (so-called because their ballpark stood at the highest point in the city at Manhattan's Hilltop Park), had a good chance of taking the American League pennant behind 41-game winner Jack Chesbro.

This one time, Boston beat out New York for the AL pennant, but the die had already been cast. There was no World Series in 1904.

Fifty-four years later, the Yankees were playing in the World Series on an almost annual basis, and the Dodgers and Giants were 3,000 miles away. Walter O'Malley, who'd forced Branch Rickey out of Brooklyn in 1950, wanted a new stadium, but not in Flushing Meadows, which was the site being offered. California was an untapped major league resource brimming with people and sunshine. Even the National Football League, a far inferior league at the time, had success with the Los Angeles Rams and San Francisco 49ers. After O'Malley urged Giants owner Horace Stoneham to join him in California, New York wound up with no National League team for the first time since 1883. New York's fierce NL rivalry was replanted on the West Coast, with O'Malley getting much better soil than Stoneham.

Meanwhile, the National League's future in New York looked bleak. The Philadelphia Phillies and Pittsburgh Pirates considered

For all he contributed to the game of baseball, Branch Rickey's role in the creation of the Mets is often overlooked.

broadcasting their games in the city, but that ended when the Yankees threatened to do the same thing in those markets. Unlike Boston, St. Louis, and Philadelphia, where the relocation of the number two teams earlier in the 1950s had actually strengthened the base of the remaining clubs in those cities, New York was never at peace with the abandonment of baseball at Ebbets Field and the Polo Grounds. The intense rivalry between the Giants and the Dodgers, plus their mutual hate for the Yankees, against whom the two teams had played 13 times in the World Series, made it impossible for many of the disenfranchised fans to even think about rooting for the AL Goliath. The Yankees' attendance actually fell in 1958, despite another world championship. (The team's turnstile count did, however, increase each year through 1961.)

TRIVIA

Which original Met modeled the team's uniform for the press in 1962?

Answers to the trivia questions are on pages 187–189.

At that time, the only way for any city to gain a major league team was to convince a franchise to move from somewhere else. There was not yet an American Football League, American Basketball Association, or World Hockey Association to point to as alternatives in sport. That would all come later.

A New York contingent led by William A. Shea tried to lure the Reds to New York, then the Pirates, but they both said no. The Phillies ignored Shea's overtures. Shea decided it would be better to start with a brand-new club rather than steal some other city's team. New Yorkers already knew how that felt.

But expansion was something that happened in *other* sports. The National League hadn't added a franchise since the collapse of the American Association in 1892, and at the turn of the century the NL had even eliminated four teams. The league rebuffed Shea's suggestion for expansion. That's when the competition card came out of the deck.

The major leagues liked competition even less than expansion. There was good reason. The National League had survived the American League threat by making peace in 1903 after two contentious years. The Federal League in 1914–15 had been a real drain

IF ONLY . . . Branch Rickey had been in his prime and willing to run the expansion Mets. He was 80 when the Mets debuted and was no longer concerned with the day-to-day dealings of a major league team. (And imagine the puzzling conversations he and Casey Stengel would have had.) When Rickey died at 83 in December 1965, the teams he'd helped give birth to in his "coat pocket" were playing in state-of-the-art facilities in Houston and, of course, New York. The clubs went on to become two success stories among the 14 expansion teams in major league history.

on both the NL and AL. While they'd ultimately defeated the Feds— and got Judge Landis and Wrigley Field out of the deal—it was not an easy time. The loss of several players to the Mexican League after World War II had also been a source of irritation.

At age 77, Branch Rickey had lived through those threats and much more. Shea asked him to be president of this new venture, the Continental League. It fed Rickey's ego while giving the league stature. Tired of doing nothing as chairman of the board for the Pirates—he'd been forced out as general manager in 1955—Rickey took on his last great challenge in the game.

Rickey was named president in August 1959, less than a month after testifying on baseball's anti-trust status in hearings held by Senator Estes Kefauver (D-Tennessee). Dismayed Pittsburgh president John Galbreath bought out Rickey, who still owned almost 1,000 shares of stock in the Pirates. The Continental League assumed the final 16 months of his contract with Pittsburgh.

While Shea had done the legwork and set up well-heeled owners in this new venture, it was Rickey who gave a swagger to this paper major league. When reporters asked where the league offices would be located, Rickey blew out smoke from his trademark cigar and said, "In my coat pocket. Where else?"

All this made good copy in the newspapers, especially in New York, with so many papers and no National League team to cover. Yet the Continental League faced real problems going forward. The minor leagues wanted millions in indemnity for losing any territory to the new league. Meanwhile, plans were in the works for a stadium in that familiar site in Flushing Meadows. There were even estimates for a moveable dome and 80,000 seats. The New York City Board of Estimate gave unanimous approval to the plans, although the dome would be better left to Continental League alum Houston.

The possibility of the Continental League ever playing a game came into question when news leaked that the AL and NL suddenly had plans of their own to expand. New York would be the new NL team, and both leagues would increase to nine teams, plus inter-league play. Quickly, though, the NL and AL contradicted each other, and other major league teams looked into relocating to sites where the Continental League had sought franchises. Rickey threatened to "raid" players in Organized Baseball, as the American League and Federal League had once done, but the master diplomat maintained contact with the major leagues. Arguments continued, Congress dismissed Kefauver's bill that might have helped the new league, and in the end there was no Continental League...but there *was* major league expansion.

A proposal by Milwaukee Braves owner Lou Perini paved the way for ownership groups from the Continental League to be admitted to the National and American leagues. From the day the idea was formed, there was no doubt that New York was the crown jewel—if not the raison d'être—for the Continental League. In this regard, they achieved victory—and Houston got a team to boot.

The New York and Houston ownership groups from the Continental League were admitted into the National League on October 17, 1960. The American League, however, shut out the Continental League, adding franchises outside the Continental

DID YOU KNOW . . . That all five of the original cities that were part of the Continental League eventually received major league teams: Minneapolis (1961), New York and Houston (1962), Toronto (1976), and Denver (1993)? Minneapolis was the only city that didn't receive an expansion franchise; it became the relocated home of the original American League Washington Senators, rechristened the Minnesota Twins.

League's ownership group. This ushered in a new Washington franchise to replace the club that was about to move to Minnesota, and Los Angeles, which eventually went to Gene Autry. The AL would start playing with 10 clubs immediately; the NL would wait until 1962. Expansion also bumped up the schedule to 162 games.

For all the maneuvering and politicking, New York got what it desperately wanted: National League baseball. Branch Rickey declined the honor of having the new stadium named after him, instead proposing that William Shea have his name stamped on the stadium. It was Shea who'd done the behind-the-scenes work, who'd gotten the idea off the ground, and, most importantly, persuaded Branch Rickey to be president of the league. Four decades later and now into a new century, Shea Stadium is the only concrete evidence of the Continental League, the most significant major league that never played a game.

Casey Calls the Tune

The original Mets should have been better. Granted, they couldn't have been any worse, but they were on a losing streak from the time they lost the coin flip in the expansion draft in Cincinnati on October 10, 1961. Although New York and Houston were the first National League franchises added since 1892, there had been expansion the previous year in the American League. The Los Angeles Angels were thrown together in a just a few months and won 70 games in 1961. The Mets won their 70th game on July 15, 1963, after they'd already lost 180 games as a franchise. How did the Mets get to be so bad? It started long before they played a game.

The Mets did have a very good ownership group, with Joan Payson leading the way. She was amazingly wealthy—*Fortune* magazine estimated her worth to be between $100 million and $200 million in 1957—and she had a knack for picking winners, whether they were horses or works of art. That ended with the Mets.

Payson was thrilled to be part of baseball again. She'd been crazy about New York Giants baseball since girlhood and she eventually owned 10 percent of the team. Hers was the lone dissenting vote on the move to San Francisco. It was Payson's backing, the work of William Shea, and the posturing of Branch Rickey that brought expansion to the National League and got New York a team to replace the Dodgers and Payson's beloved Giants. That turned out to be the last thing that went right for several years.

The Mets went for names over potential. The two men they chose to put a quality product on the field—George Weiss and Casey Stengel—certainly had plenty of experience. Weiss had built the Yankees' farm system and turned it into a machine where All-Stars were commonly replaced by Hall of Famers. When he was named general manager of the Yankees, he elevated Stengel from the minor leagues to manage the Yankees in 1949. Stengel was seen in some circles as a clown, as someone who'd been given plenty of chances yet had exactly one winning season out of nine with the Dodgers and Braves. Given top-notch talent, Stengel won the World Series in each of his first five years as manager of the Yankees. He won five more pennants, but three World Series defeats—culminating with a disastrous loss to an inferior Pittsburgh club in 1960—sent Weiss and Stengel out the door. Weiss was 65 when M. Donald Grant, a stockbroker acting on the owner's behalf, hired him to run the Mets; Stengel was 71 when Weiss pulled him out of retirement.

If the story was scripted, this is where the two great men who'd been told they were too old by the crosstown bully would hitch up their belts and put together one final, great showing just to prove 'em wrong. Reality intervened. The 1962 Mets were the worst team of the modern era while the Yankees steamrolled to another world championship.

There was no free agency to help a club back then, and the expansion draft did little more than provide warm bodies, and not necessarily that. During four hours of the draft, the Mets spent $1.8 million to purchase 22 players. The names still seem familiar because of all the outlandish exploits they would have in the inaugural year: Choo Choo Coleman, Jay Hook, Felix Mantilla, Gus Bell, unlucky Craig Anderson, and even more unfortunate Roger Craig. There were names that would harbor future promise: Al Jackson, who would become a fixture in the organization and have two decent seasons jammed between a pair of 8–20 campaigns, and Gil

DID YOU KNOW . . . That Mets announcer Lindsey Nelson broadcast a game from a gondola under the roof of the brand-new Astrodome on April 28, 1965? Unlucky Lindsey was the only announcer in the room as Mets TV producer Joe Gallagher made arrangements to wire the gondola for sound 208 feet above second base. Even from way up there, Nelson could still clearly see another bad night for the 112-loss Mets.

In Casey Stengel, the circus that was the 1962 Mets had its ringleader.

Hodges, who would become the team's greatest manager, but as a player, he was done. There were a lot of those types of ballplayers in the Mets' early years. Duke Snider, Yogi Berra, Warren Spahn, Hall of Famers all, but they were brought to the Mets as if they were guest stars on *Bonanza*, ready to ride into the sunset. Richie Ashburn was another future Hall of Famer, but he actually contributed. He was the team's first All-Star and led the 1962 club in walks and hitting while tying Elio Chacon for the club lead with 12 stolen bases. Ashburn enjoyed the season so much that he retired when it was over. His long career as a broadcaster, however, was enhanced by his ability to break out original Mets stories during any rain delay or 10-run deficit.

The 1962 Mets were a joke, but that was all right because they were led by Casey Stengel, who'd reverted to the clown everyone thought he was going to be back in '49. Although the Mets stunk up the old Polo Grounds, people were just thrilled to have the place back in use and a National League club back in the city. Great stars came to New York for the first time in years: Hank Aaron, Eddie Mathews, Frank Robinson, and Ernie Banks, plus Sandy Koufax and Don Drysdale, who'd become stars in L.A. And, of course, seeing Willie Mays back at the Polo Grounds was worth the $3.50 for a box seat. If you came to see the Mets, well, you had to alter your taste to the bizarre.

Although Hodges hit the franchise's first home run and set a short-lived National League record for most career homers by a right-handed hitter, a month into his Mets tenure the team needed a replacement. On May 9, the club acquired its quintessential player, a man whose initials even spelled MET: Marvin Eugene Throneberry. The one-time Yankee had been traded to the A's as part of the Roger Maris deal in 1959, but Marvelous Marv gave the '62 Mets everything he had. He made just 17 errors over parts of six other seasons in the majors, but he committed 17 miscues with the original Mets. His first-inning error on June 17 allowed Lou Brock, then a Cub, to come up with two outs. He homered to the distant center field bleachers at the Polo Grounds. In the bottom of the inning, Throneberry tripled in two runs but was called out for missing first base. As Casey Stengel came out to argue, first base coach Cookie Lavagetto told him, "Forget it Casey, he missed second, too." The next batter, Charlie Neal, homered, and the Mets wound up losing by a run. Because it was that kind of year,

TRIVIA

Which Met became the first to start in a midsummer classic?

Answers to the trivia questions are on pages 187–189.

they lost the second game that day as well, with Throneberry booting a grounder hit by the leadoff batter.

Frank Thomas hit 34 home runs and nearly drove in 100 runs, but his year still had the requisite oddness required of all original Mets. On April 29 he was hit by pitches twice in one inning. That it tied a record was one thing, but what made it "amazin'," as Casey loved to say, was that it helped the Mets win consecutive games for the first time in history. It didn't last long; they lost the second game that day.

The Mets lost their 100th game with August still on the calendar. They didn't slow down after that, losing 20 of their final 26 decisions

DID YOU KNOW . . . That among the finalists for the name of the club were "Bees," "Burros," "Continentals," "Skyscrapers," "Jets," as well as the eventual runner-up, "Skyliners"? Owner Joan Payson held a preference for "Meadowlarks," but the organization chose "Mets," mainly because it was actually part of its existing corporate name: New York Metropolitan Baseball Club, Incorporated. Like most good sports nicknames, though, it had already been used. The New York Metropolitans of the long-defunct American Association were the first team in that league to play the National League in a "World Series" (far inferior to the World Series started between the AL and NL in 1903). As newspaper editors had found during those Mets' five-season run in the 19th century, the name fit well in a headline. And in the first years, the NL Mets were also good for a punch line.

to accumulate the most losses of the century. Only the 1899 Cleveland Spiders, dealing with syndicate ownership, facing contraction, and playing just 41 times at home in front of an average of 150 fans per game, beat out the Mets for the most losses ever. But while the 20–134 Spiders were squashed out of existence after the season, the Mets rolled on, racking up 231 losses in two years while calling the Polo Grounds home.

Roger Craig, the patron saint of unlucky Mets, lost the first game in franchise history on his way to 24 losses in '62, but he still deferred to Craig Anderson's club record of 16 straight losses—for a year. In 1963 Craig dropped an NL record-tying 18 straight, with the Mets scoring just 29 runs for him over the stretch. The mark would last until Anthony Young, who had the kind of luck that would've made him an ideal original Met, broke it 30 years later.

The Mets stunk up brand-new Shea Stadium with 109 and 112 defeats their first two years there, and they even lost Casey Stengel along the way. The night before the 1965 Old Timer's Game, Stengel broke his hip while reveling at Toots Shor's. He didn't really even feel the pain until the next morning. The on-field pain was over, though. A month later, the "Old Perfessor," now 75 and more somber than usual, still joked that he very well couldn't walk to the mound and take out a pitcher while leaning on a cane. Despite the worst record any manager has ever logged in three and a half seasons, Stengel still

By the
NUMBERS

37—Casey Stengel's No. 37 was the first uniform number retired by the Mets. Both the Mets and Yankees retired the number in honor of the Hall of Fame. His 37 is the only number between 0 and 59 never worn by a Mets player.

retired with a winning career record and a tie with his mentor John McGraw for most pennants won, with 10.

Wes Westrum, who'd filled in for Stengel since the accident, took over as manager on a full-time basis. The former catcher had actually been acquired by the Mets in a coach-for-coach swap with San Francisco: Lavagetto for Westrum, straight up. Stengel had taken a shine to Westrum after the two met late at night in a bar during the 1963 All-Star break in Cleveland. The Mets selected Westrum as Stengel's replacement over Yogi Berra, who had managed the Yankees to a pennant a year earlier. Either way, the Mets were bound to end up with a manager known for his malapropisms. Although no Yogi in any corner—Westrum once called a tight game "a real cliff dweller"—he would bring the Mets to their first season without 100 losses and out of last place, all the way to ninth place in 1966. "Baseball is like church," Westrum said. "Many attend, few understand." The first five seasons in Mets history were better off not understood.

Stumbling on the Franchise

Tom Seaver is the best pitcher in Mets history. That statement was true during Seaver's rookie season of 1967. It's still true four decades later. While Tom Terrific's success came from hard work, God-given talent, and brains, the fact that he was a Met at all was pure luck.

George Thomas Seaver was the fourth child of Charlie and Betty Seaver. Charlie, the California amateur golf champion in the 1930s, went to Stanford University and later worked as an engineer. Tom inherited the sports bloodline and was always a fine athlete, yet he wasn't considered major league material at Fresno High School. He went into the marines and then attended Fresno City Community College. Seaver had filled out during his time in the service and threw the ball harder than he ever had in high school. That, matched with his pinpoint control, brought him to the attention of legendary USC coach Ron Dedeaux. After just one year as a Trojan, Seaver already displayed major league talent. The Braves were watching. Seaver should have, by all rights, been the first great move by that club following their relocation from Milwaukee to Atlanta. Who says the Braves have all the luck?

Seaver was available in the special January 1966 draft of players who had once been drafted but not signed. The Dodgers had picked Seaver in the 10th round of the first-ever draft in 1965, but he opted for USC. The Mets selected and signed another hard thrower two rounds later in that inaugural draft: Nolan Ryan.

The Braves picked Seaver in the 1966 special draft and then signed him. The problem was, the signing took place two days after USC's season had begun. That violated the rules set up between Organized Baseball and the NCAA. With Seaver ineligible to return to

The arrival of Tom Seaver ushered in a new era of hope, and things miraculously turned around for the Mets.

USC to pitch because of NCAA rules, commissioner William Eckert voided the contract and announced that a special lottery would be held for the rights to Seaver's services. To claim the prize, the winner had to match the $45,000 the Braves had offered. It remains the lone memorable decision made during the four-year term of William Eckert, a former general and the blandest commissioner on record. Derided by critics as the "Unknown Soldier," Eckert inadvertently provided the Mets with their first true stroke of luck as a franchise.

The man who deserved credit for giving the Mets a shot at Seaver was assistant general manager Bing Devine. According to the Mets by the Numbers website, it was Devine who convinced club president George Weiss to enter the lottery. A good workout for the

Indians front office helped persuade Weiss to at least let the Mets take a chance on Seaver. The shock was that only three teams took the trouble to enter the April 3 lottery (the Braves weren't allowed and the Dodgers were no longer interested). The Mets were chosen over Cleveland and Philadelphia for the rights to Seaver. Weiss gulped and forked over the $45,000.

The Mets assigned Seaver to Jacksonville of the Southern League and kept a close eye on him. A year after the Mets hit the lottery with the Fresno phenom, Weiss had retired, Devine was the GM, and Tom Seaver was on the major league roster.

In his third career start, Seaver took a 1–0 lead into the bottom of the ninth at Wrigley Field. An error by Bud Harrelson tied the score, but Seaver got out of the inning, led off the tenth with a single, and came around to score on a hit by Al Luplow. He retired the Cubs in order in the tenth, throwing just 111 pitches for the first of his 231 career complete games (171 as a Met). The team was still bad, but the confident 22-year-old didn't want to hear any laugh-out-loud tales about finding new ways to lose. To Seaver, there was nothing funny about it.

"There was an aura of defeatism and I refused to accept it," Seaver later said. "Maybe some of the others started to feel how I felt because I noticed that the team started to play better behind me than it did for any other pitcher."

Seaver's 16 wins and 2.76 ERA as a 22-year-old rookie was by far the best season put up by anyone to that point in franchise history. Best of all, Seaver was durable. In the days when managers often confused pitch count with pitch out and completing games was a matter of course, Seaver didn't exit a game without a good reason. He started 34 times as a rookie and completed 18, logging 251 innings. It was the first of 10 straight years as a Met he threw 200 or more innings. His 170 strikeouts as a rookie marked the only year in that period in which he didn't fan at least 200 batters.

He also pitched the final inning of the longest All-Star Game in history, tossing a scoreless fifteenth in a 2–1

TRIVIA

Who did the Mets take with the second overall pick in the first amateur draft in 1965?

Answers to the trivia questions are on pages 187–189.

By the NUMBERS **11**—Number of Mets in the National Baseball Hall of Fame. Tom Seaver was the first Met elected to Cooperstown based mainly on his accomplishments with the club, but 10 others have joined the Hall of Fame with some Mets experience on their résumés. Their years with the Mets are listed after their name, and their year of induction is in parentheses. (Yogi Berra was voted into the Hall of Fame as a catcher, so his years as Mets manager aren't included.) VC stands for election by the Veteran's Committee. In addition, two Mets announcers have been honored with the Ford C. Frick and are part of a permanent display at the Hall of Fame: Lindsey Nelson (1988) and Bob Murphy (1994).

Name	Position	Year(s) as Met	Year Elected
Casey Stengel	Manager	1962–1965	(1966, VC)
George Weiss	Executive	1962–1966	(1971, VC)
Richie Ashburn	OF	1962	(1995, VC)
Duke Snider	OF	1963	(1980)
Warren Spahn	P	1965	(1973)
Yogi Berra	C	1965	(1972)
Nolan Ryan	P	1966, 1968–1971	(1999)
Tom Seaver	P	1967–1977, 1983	(1992)
Willie Mays	OF	1972–1973	(1979)
Gary Carter	C	1985–1989	(2003)
Eddie Murray	1B	1992–1993	(2003)

National League victory in Anaheim. He struck out Ken Berry to end the game. The other players in the NL clubhouse were impressed with this rookie, who was the first Mets pitcher to be invited to the All-Star Game and probably the first hurler the club ever had who earned more respect than sympathy. Seaver easily claimed National League Rookie of the Year despite playing on the team with the worst record in baseball.

Seaver worked beautifully with catcher Jerry Grote. The Mets had picked up the reticent backstop from the Astros in 1965 for Tom

Parsons, who'd gone 1–10 in his lone full season in New York and never pitched for Houston. Grote batted just .195 in 1967, but for the first time in a pitcher-friendly decade, the Mets pulled their ERA under 4.00. So they let Grote catch 120 games, even with his paltry hitting. His batting would improve and, more importantly, the pitching staff started to blossom. Almost everyone seemed to pitch well to Grote. It might have been his soft hands and drill sergeant demeanor behind the plate, and it might have been that they were good pitchers working in a tough park to hit in. All they had to do was ask Grote about Shea being tough on hitters.

To the shock of the National League, facing the Mets was starting to become a chore, although opponents still usually left with a victory. Don Cardwell, a 31-year-old veteran with a high ERA, came to the Mets in 1967 and lowered his ERA to 3.57; his ERA would go down each of his first two years with the Mets. Relief specialist Ron Taylor, a veteran of the 1964 world champion Cardinals, came to the Mets in '67 and produced the lowest ERA of his career at 2.34. Bullpen mate Cal Koonce, after middling results as a Cub, was purchased from Chicago in August, and his improvement was immediate. The significance of both Taylor and Koonce would grow over the coming seasons. Jerry Koosman, who debuted in 1967, would better Seaver's first-year numbers in 1968, but he'd lose the NL Rookie of the Year trophy by one vote to a revolutionary catcher from Cincinnati named Johnny Bench.

Yet for all this, Mets baseball in the 1967 "Summer of Love" was about falling for Tom Seaver. Bing Devine and the Mets had gambled on the rookie, and they'd hit the lottery, literally. He even outlasted his manager—Wes Westrum resigned in September and let Salty Parker absorb the team's 100th defeat, a 3–0 loss by Seaver against Claude Osteen and the Dodgers. It might have seemed like yet another brutal season in the standings for the sad-sack Mets, but this time there was actually something there: the Franchise.

Seaver would dominate the club's record book as well as National League opponents over the next decade. He won the Cy Young Award in 1969, 1973, and 1975, the first right-hander to do so. Seaver somehow finished second to Ferguson Jenkins in 1971 despite winning 20 games and leading the NL with 289 strikeouts; his

That in 1975, the year he won his third Cy Young Award, Tom Seaver became the first pitcher in baseball history to fan 200 batters for eight straight years? He extended his record to nine the next season, but the streak ended the year he was traded to Cincinnati in 1977.

1.76 ERA was a full run lower than the Cubs hurler, who allowed the most hits and home runs, but the baseball writers salivated over Fergie's 24 wins. (Seaver the Red would likewise be robbed of the Cy Young in 1981 because of voters' infatuation with Fernando Valenzuela.) Seaver finished second in NL MVP voting in 1969, and he remains the only Met to earn *Sports Illustrated*'s Sportsman of the Year. Seaver would dominate every significant pitching category in club history, become the only Mets player to have his number retired, and pontificate on all matters Mets for seven seasons as a broadcaster for the club. He generated the highest percentile vote in Hall of Fame history (98.84) when he was elected in 1992, becoming the only man wearing a Mets cap on his Cooperstown plaque. Seaver received the most votes of five Mets in the Major League Baseball's "Hometown Heroes" promotion in 2006. Like there was ever any doubt.

Yet if not for a bit of luck and a relocating club's tardiness in handling his contract, Seaver might have done many of these feats as a Brave. Seaver did get to pitch the first ever National League Championship Series game before 50,000 in Atlanta in 1969. Of course, he did it wearing "New York" on his chest, and of course he beat them.

The Greatest: Gil Hodges

No manager has been as important to the Mets franchise as Gil Hodges. Without Hodges, the Mets might have become the Washington Senators, a team whose losing grew so tiresome even Ted Williams couldn't save them from running to Texas. Hodges knew all about the Senators. That's where he came from.

Beloved as a Brooklyn Dodger, and adequate as a Los Angeles Dodger, the Mets plucked Hodges from L.A.'s roster in the expansion draft and later traded him to the Senators for Jimmy Piersall in May 1963. Ailing Hodges retired as a player and immediately became Washington's manager. His best season with the Senators was 76 wins and sixth place in a 10-team league. Washington traded him to the Mets for $100,000 and Bill Denehy, who had a 1–7 mark as a Mets rookie in 1967; Denehy never increased that win total.

Not included in the deal but a key component nonetheless was Rube Walker, who left the Senators and joined the Mets. A teammate of Hodges's in Brooklyn, the former catcher worked exceedingly well with young pitchers. The Mets that Hodges inherited were an absolute mess, but pitching talent was brimming in the minor leagues. Having worked with the struggling Senators, Hodges—and Walker—learned firsthand how to instill confidence even as the team crumbled and fumbled around them. It was assumed that the pitchers, and everyone else, had a strong work ethic. If they didn't, they wouldn't be around long.

Hodges survived a mild heart attack at the end of the 1968 season, and the Mets held off Houston to keep out of last place for the second time in franchise history. New York also avoided 90 losses for the first time ever. The team's ERA was 2.72, fourth best in the

DID YOU KNOW . . . That Tommie Agee's second sensational diving catch in Game 3 of the 1969 World Series rescued Nolan Ryan in the lone World Series appearance of his illustrious 27-year career? Ryan had just relieved starter Gary Gentry with the bases loaded and two outs in the seventh, but Paul Blair's shot was caught as Agee slid on his belly in right-center. (Agee earlier robbed Elrod Hendricks with an acrobatic backhanded catch with two on in the fourth.) Ryan earned the save.

league. Granted, it was the "Year of the Pitcher," and the NL as a whole had an ERA under 3.00, but this was clearly progress. The original Mets, the '62 laughingstock that Hodges had played for, had an ERA of 5.04. The '68 club allowed the fewest hits in the NL. Rookie Jerry Koosman just missed 20 wins while allowing 7.54 hits and 2.08 earned runs per nine innings. Tom Seaver won 16 games for the second straight year and at 23 was already thinking like a veteran. The whole team would grow up quickly in 1969.

Hodges refused to be surprised when halfway through the season the Mets were 12 games over .500 and within striking distance of the Cubs. He expected his players to comport themselves like professionals; he expected opponents to act that way, too. When Hodges met Cubs captain Ron Santo at home plate to exchange lineup cards before the July 15 game at Wrigley Field, the Chicago third baseman explained that his annoying habit of clicking his heels after wins was something the Wrigley fans demanded. Hodges told Santo the parable of Tug McGraw: "When he was young and immature and nervous, he used to jump up and down. He doesn't do it anymore." He left Santo standing alone at home plate, and his team went out and won that day and the next. Santo and the Cubs did not click their heels in front of the Mets again in 1969. Their next win against New York came on the last day of the season, more than a week after the Mets had clinched the division title the Cubs seemingly had wrapped up in July.

A few faint voices spoke against Hodges, but those were back in Washington. The loudest voice belonged to opinionated former Senator Ken "Hawk" Harrelson. He called the manager "unfair, unreasonable, unfeeling, incapable of handling men, stubborn, holier-than-thou, and ice-cold," but Hodges could do no wrong in New York. In a September 1969 piece in *Time* magazine, Koosman said of his manager: "Hodges is one hell of a leader. He always has time to talk to you, he has a good sense of humor, and if he's distant, it's because he never wants to embarrass himself or the team. I wouldn't trade Hodges for any two other managers."

The son of an Indiana coalminer, Hodges was a marine sergeant—and Bronze Star recipient—for action in the South Pacific during World War II. He always got his point across. Hodges wasn't a yeller and didn't make idle threats, but he was among the most respected people in baseball from the day he debuted in the major leagues in 1943 until he died in a golf course parking lot in front of his coaching staff three decades later.

Hodges was never booed in Brooklyn—a feat in itself—and was worshipped by Mets fans. He loved kids, attended church devoutly, and, in the heat of the first pennant race in Mets history, he calmly went out to left field in the middle of an inning and removed his best everyday player.

With the Mets getting pounded at Shea in the midst of a 10-run inning in the second game of a doubleheader

TRIVIA

The Mets have long been known more for pitching than for hitting, but how many years did it take the club before it batted higher than .250 in a season?

Answers to the trivia questions are on pages 187–189.

sweep by the Astros on July 30, Cleon Jones loafed after Johnny Edwards's second hit of the frame as a run scored. Hodges stepped out of the dugout and started walking. He passed Nolan Ryan, whom he had just brought in to pitch, and he kept on going until he reached Jones in left field. Hodges asked about his player's health and after a few more words they both walked off the field, with Jones several paces behind his manager. Ron Swoboda took over in left. Ryan was so shocked, he allowed a homer to the next batter, pitcher Larry Dierker. The Mets lost—and were outscored by Houston on the day, 27–8—but New York, six and a half games behind the Cubs at the end of that series, went 45–16 from that point on. Although Tom Seaver lost the series finale to the Astros (the only team the '69 Mets had a losing record against), he went 10–1 down the stretch. Cleon

TOP 10

Best Mets Managers

1. Gil Hodges

Having the Miracle Mets on your résumé is enough to be number one. Hodges instilled discipline and confidence simultaneously. He turned a laughingstock franchise into a team that thrived on pitching, platooning, and pluck. The 1970s might have been so different at Shea had he lived.

2. Davey Johnson

Brought the team from the sewer and transformed the Mets into an immediate force. He treated the Mets like men, and they played like it. Five bittersweet endings—plus one remarkably thrilling finish—produced the most wins of any Mets manager and a .588 winning percentage.

3. Bobby Valentine

He took players no one wanted and made them reliable regulars at discount prices. After an unforgettable 1999 finish, he raised the stakes in 2000 with a bail-and-wire outfield that stole a pennant. He had trouble with the Braves and Yankees, but Bobby V. made other managerial "geniuses" like Dusty Baker and Tony La Russa look like amateurs.

4. Yogi Berra

He slides in at number four because he won one of the most unlikely pennants in major league history with the '73 club. He put in plenty of time as a coach with the Mets before he replaced Hodges under tragic circumstances just before the 1972 season.

5. Willie Randolph

Some question his in-game managing skills, but the team has his respect and his back. While the Mets went down the tubes late in 2003 and 2004, Randolph's first club bounced back and finished the '05 season strong to knock three division rivals out of playoff contention and sound the bell for the dominance of '06.

6. Casey Stengel
*No Mets manager has ever—or heaven help us, will ever—
eclipse his franchise-low .302 winning percentage, although
Valentine, Johnson, and Joe Torre surpassed his 404 losses.
Casey made people talk about the Mets from the day he was
hired, even if the people were laughing.*

7. Dallas Green
*A hard-edged guy you didn't want against you, he took over
the Torborg/Harazin disaster and stuck with the kids. He
played rookies over veterans, including 22-year-old Edgardo
Alfonzo in 1995 when he couldn't hit a ball to the left of
second base. Green didn't mince words, and he probably
should've tried that.*

8. Joe Torre
*People often say that Torre didn't have the horses to win with the
Mets, but he didn't ride the horses he had particularly well,
either. He was the only player/manager in franchise history—
that lasted about a week—and the Mets never finished closer
than 24 games back except during the strike season, when they
barely surpassed the 40 wins of the 1962 club.*

9. Joe Frazier
*Had a good first season with a veteran club, but when adversity
kicked in the next year he panicked and the team foundered. He
should never have been hired as manager.*

10. Bud Harrelson
See Joe Frazier.

Jones? He wound up hitting .340—a mark unsurpassed by a Met for
almost 30 years—and quickly hustled his way back into his
manager's good graces. In fact, one of Hodges's most memorable
moments took place with Jones at bat.

By October 16, 1969, the city was absolutely giddy over the Mets.
They had overtaken the Cubs for the division title, swept the Braves
in the first Championship Series, and used every manner of highlight
reel play to win three straight from the dominant Orioles in the
World Series after losing the opener. Still, the Mets trailed the

Gil Hodges, shown here examining the famous shoe-polish ball with umpire Lou DiMuro in the 1969 World Series, was the perfect leader for the young Mets during that amazing season.

Orioles in the sixth inning, 3–0, as Dave McNally allowed only two hits and two walks. An inside pitch by McNally bounced past Jones's left foot and umpire Lou DiMuro immediately threw another ball into play. McNally was deciding on his next pitch to Jones when Hodges appeared with a ball that had shoe polish on it. DiMuro looked at the evidence and sent Jones to first base. (That the same thing had happened to Nippy Jones a dozen World Series earlier or that Frank Robinson had been hit by a pitch and DiMuro had not seen it earlier in the inning were beside the point.)

Donn Clendenon followed with a home run to left. Al Weis, part of a platoon system Hodges used at three different positions, homered to tie the game in the seventh. Jones started a rally in the eighth, and platoon player Swoboda—whose phenomenal catch saved Game 4—knocked in the go-ahead run. Koosman completed the miracle with a scoreless ninth in Game 5.

The 1969 Mets had unbelievable—all right, amazin'—pitching. New York tossed 28 shutouts and allowed barely one base runner per inning. Their 51 complete games were only fifth in the league, but Hodges used his bullpen magnificently behind Tug McGraw, Ron Taylor, Cal Koonce, and swingman Nolan Ryan. Hodges had a lot of pitchers to choose from—he had two of the best young starters in the game in Seaver and Koosman, and Gary Gentry was the third Mets rookie in as many years to have an outstanding debut season— but the club's hitters were ordinary at best. Import Clendenon provided power while Jones and Tommie Agee were steady, yet the team hit just two points better than the expansion Expos and scored 88 fewer times than the Cubs and 93 runs less than the third-place Pirates. Only four NL teams hit fewer home runs. Hodges used everybody on his bench, putting them in situations where they could succeed. Leo Durocher's Cubs, meanwhile, had one set lineup. When the Cubs hit the skids under the hot Chicago sun, the worn-out players had nothing left.

The Mets couldn't sustain the miracle in the years to come. They finished third with 83 wins each of the next two years. The pitching remained superb, but the collection of castoffs and mediocre home-grown talent in the lineup only had so many hits in them. Hodges died while the luster of his achievement was still felt in every corner of Shea Stadium. Fittingly, his number was retired.

"My main goal was to change the notion that everything the Mets did was wrong," Hodges said. "I wanted them to do things right."

Kooz

Jerry Koosman is the greatest left-hander ever developed by the Mets. While that statement does not take into account the end-of-career exploits of Tom Glavine and Warren Spahn, or the potential future success of one Scott Kazmir, what makes Kooz stand out is that nothing was expected of him...except that he repay a loan.

Koosman was signed in 1964, the year before the first amateur draft, but he was by no means a bonus baby. The Minnesota native had excelled in army competition and was looked at by the Twins. The Mets were interested because the son of John Luchese, a Shea Stadium usher, had played with the southpaw in the service at Fort Bliss, Texas. By 1964 it was quite apparent that anyone who could throw a baseball—and keep someone from hitting it a long way—would get a chance with the Mets. The Twins had pitchers Jim Kaat, Mudcat Grant, Jim Perry, and Camilo Pascual, an All-Star coming off consecutive 20-win seasons. Although the Twins first offered $10,000 and the Mets $1,600, Koosman was intrigued by opportunity over money. Each time he got back in touch with the Mets, they lowered their offer by $100. His famous line: "I figured I'd better sign before I owed them money."

In time, Koosman did owe the team money, for a car loan. At the same time, he was having too much fun and not pitching well in Class A. Rather than cut him and never get their money back, the Mets kept him around, hoping he'd at least make good on the loan. Patience paid off.

Koosman had a 1.38 ERA in 170 innings to lead the New York–Penn League. The next year he led the International League in strikeouts. Just as Koosman planned, he was in New York's starting rotation quickly. After just three seasons in the minors, he was not only earning a major league paycheck, but he set the franchise mark with 19 victories and tied the National League rookie mark with seven shutouts, last reached by Grover Cleveland Alexander in 1911. He missed the Rookie of the Year Award by one vote—the closest margin to that point—to Reds catcher Johnny Bench. Koosman fanned Carl Yastrzemski to end the NL's 1–0 All-Star victory in Houston. Playing with teammates Tom Seaver and Jerry Grote, it marked the first time more than the required one Met made the All-Star team.

Koosman and Seaver gave the Mets a formidable left–right combo capable of competing with any team in the league. But with the 1969 club off to an unimpressive 7–11 start, Koosman left the first Mets game ever played in Montreal with a dead arm. Some feared he might never be the same pitcher, but after nearly a month off he returned looking more alive than ever. Koosman finished with 17 victories as the Amazin' Mets, who averaged 105 losses in their

Southpaw Jerry Koosman joined Tom Seaver in the rotation to form one of the most reliable lefty-righty combos in the big leagues.

All-1960s Mets Team

Position	Name
First Baseman	Donn Clendenon
Second Baseman	Ron Hunt
Shortstop	Bud Harrelson
Third Baseman	Ed Charles
Left Fielder	Cleon Jones
Center Fielder	Tommie Agee
Right Fielder	Ron Swoboda
Catcher	Jerry Grote
Right-handed Pitcher	Tom Seaver
Left-handed Pitcher	Jerry Koosman
Relief Pitcher	Ron Taylor
Overlooked Pitcher	Al Jackson
Utility Player	Ed Kranepool
Manager	Gil Hodges

first seven seasons of existence, actually won 100 games. Koosman's last outing produced his 13th career shutout in just his 69th start in the big leagues.

Koosman made up for the missed time in the postseason. Although he was knocked out of his NLCS start, the Mets won, anyway. The seven hits he allowed in Atlanta matched the total number he would allow in two World Series starts. They are still probably the two best starts by a Met in World Series competition.

The Orioles blasted Seaver, as everyone predicted, in the first game of the '69 Series. Koosman took the mound the next day at Memorial Stadium and pitched no-hit ball for six innings. He surrendered a single to Paul Blair to start the seventh, and Brooks Robinson later got the second and last hit off Kooz to tie the game. After Al Weis singled home the go-ahead run with two outs in the top of the ninth—while weak-hitting Koosman waited on deck—Kooz retired the first two batters in the ninth. He walked the next two. Ron Taylor came in to get the last out as the Mets evened the Series.

Two more shocking victories followed, and Koosman took the mound in Game 5 at Shea with the improbable assignment of finishing the miracle. It looked bad in the third inning when—thinking bunt with a man on first—Kooz grooved a pitch that opposing hurler Dave McNally whacked into the left-field bullpen. Frank Robinson added a solo shot before the inning was done for a 3–0 lead. But Kooz allowed just one more hit that Thursday afternoon, giving the Mets time to fashion some more magic. The Cleon Jones shoe-polish incident, followed immediately by Donn Clendenon's home run, made it a one-run game. Al Weis hit an unlikely game-tying homer. A Ron Swoboda RBI-double and two Baltimore errors on one play made it 5–3 in the eighth. Koosman followed that by walking the leadoff man in the ninth.

Boog Powell, Brooks Robinson, and Davey Johnson, the four-five-six hitters for a 109-win powerhouse club, were due up. Powell, with 37 homers and 121 RBIs during the year, hit into a force play. Brooks Robinson, whose liner had seemingly won the previous day's game—only to be turned into a game-tying sacrifice fly on Swoboda's diving catch—hit a much easier fly to Swoboda this time. That brought up Davey Johnson, who would, of course, one day manage the Mets to their second world championship. He hit a fly ball near the warning track in left. By the time Jones caught it and took a knee, Koosman was in Grote's arms, Ed Charles was dancing, and fans were flooding the field.

Despite some physical ailments and ineffectiveness in the early 1970s, Koosman accumulated 104 more wins as a Met (good for 140 in orange and blue). He set a still-standing club mark of 31⅔ consecutive scoreless innings during the Mets' 1973 pennant push. He endured five straight losses before starting his streak on August 19 and reeling off four straight wins, three by shutout. He went on to earn a win in both the 1973 NLCS and World Series (he never lost a postseason game in seven career appearances). Koosman had a 21-win season for the Mets in 1976, finishing second in the Cy Young voting. Then it all disintegrated.

TRIVIA

Who was the youngest Met to homer in a game?

Answers to the trivia questions are on pages 187–189.

While the twosome of Seaver and Koosman had become a power trio with hard-throwing lefty Jon Matlack, the front office debacle in the years immediately following the death of original owner Joan Payson led to the stripping of the franchise for spare parts. Seaver, the face of the Mets, and Dave Kingman, the only hitter left to strike any fear in opponents, were traded the same horrible June night in 1977. Matlack, Grote, John Milner, and almost anyone else of value had disappeared by the start of '78. Except for Koosman.

Kooz absorbed innings and defeats for the NL's worst team. He went from 20-game winner to 20-game loser, and played luckless opponent in Seaver's first game at Shea wearing another team's uniform on August 21, 1977. The Mets scored just one run that day for Koosman. He went 3–15 the next year and threatened to retire if the Mets didn't trade him to Minnesota. He'd made the right choice to sign with the Mets 15 years earlier; now he needed to escape before his 137 losses as a Met—the only major category with his name at the top—grew exponentially. Koosman won 20 his first year as a Twin and later pitched for the White Sox and Phillies on his way to 82 non-Mets victories in the big leagues.

Koosman would always be remembered at Shea, though, for his fastball in on the hands, then a big curve, and smiling on *Kiner's Korner* with a towel wrapped around his neck after it was over. The Mets had been both lucky and smart to keep Kooz around back in 1966. He paid back the loan in full.

Screwball Tug

Before the Mets ever had any thing to be exuberant about, Tug McGraw couldn't contain himself. He was so excited about striking out Orlando Cepeda in his major league debut that the trainer had to give Tug a tranquilizer. They later had to give him a tranquilizer before a start, but he didn't fare too well. He was just 2–7 as a 20-year-old rookie in 1965—although one of those wins came against Sandy Koufax—and Tug followed that with an accelerated stint in the marines that kept him with the Mets and out of Vietnam. Then he came back and hurt his arm.

Over the next two seasons, Tug pitched just four times for the Mets, but in the minors he slowly began to master his control, plus a pitch that Ralph Terry had taught him on a golf course during an Instructional League stint: the screwball. It says something about the quality of an organization's instructors that a player and not a coach introduced Tug to the pitch that changed his career. Tug had to work on it in secret at various times to keep away from disapproving instructors. Gil Hodges eventually let him throw the pitch, and it helped change the franchise's fate.

Tug had been used mainly as a starter, but with a rotation that included Tom Seaver, Jerry Koosman, and Gary Gentry, plus several more hard throwers awaiting a chance, Hodges decided to have Tug work out of the bullpen for the '69 club. With Ron Taylor, Cal Koonce, and a kid named Nolan Ryan sitting around, it was a formidable pen. McGraw went 9–3, pitched 100 innings, appeared 42 times, had a 2.24 ERA, and went 12-for-12 in saves the first year it was an official statistic. He pitched in the first NLCS, and his strikeout of Hank Aaron in Game 2 provided "the confidence I would ride the rest of my career." The slapping his thigh with his glove? That just came naturally.

Although Tug did not appear in the World Series victory over the Orioles, 1969 went pretty well for a guy who'd been left unprotected the previous fall in the early rounds of the expansion draft for the Padres and Expos. Tug quickly became one of the most beloved stars in New York. The charismatic southpaw's life in a Mets uniform was about a lot more than just what happened on the field. Some music, maestro.

- He cut hair for the homeless in the Bowery.
- His dog, Pucci (call him Poochie), dug up the flowers outside the team's executive office during spring training in 1968. The dog later left a present outside Joe Pignatano's room that the coach didn't see until it was too late. Tug was sent to the minors.
- Ron Taylor slapped him during a public relations tour in Vietnam for smoking marijuana.
- He came up with a way to measure the effectiveness of a relief pitcher, a plus and minus system that took into account several different statistics for relievers. It didn't catch on.
- He sprained his ankle on a toboggan run with Ron Swoboda during the winter of 1970 and came up with the excuse that he was injured slipping on ice while taking out the garbage.
- Going back to his year in junior college before signing with the Mets, Tug dislocated a finger on his pitching hand jumping out of a hay barn, and also suffered a cracked vertebrae playing football in JC.

Yet, Tug wouldn't have been a Met at all if not for his older brother, Hank, who signed with the Mets out of high school in Vallejo, California. Hank asked Roy Partee, the Mets scout who signed him, to look at Tug after everyone else lost interest following a lousy junior college tournament performance. Hank never made the Mets—although his hardheaded ways often made the Mets angry—but his brother turned into an All-Star.

An impromptu lesson on a golf course changed Tug McGraw's career—and the fate of the Mets.

Tug had a 1.70 ERA in 1971 and again in 1972, and he earned the win in the '72 All-Star Game in Atlanta. His 27 saves that year remained the club record until Jesse Orosco broke it in 1984. But what everyone remembers about Tug McGraw, and the salutation he used for the rest of his life, is three simple words: "Ya Gotta Believe."

A motivational speaker friend came up with the mantra when Tug and the Mets were in the dumps in the summer of 1973. Tug started saying it...a lot. When team president M. Donald Grant gave a speech to the slumping club—"it took 20 minutes to say what should have taken five"—Tug cut him off after Grant said he still believed in the team. Tug started shouting, "Ya gotta believe," over and over. An angry Grant, assuming he was being mocked, was wrong once again. Tug was serious, and he told Grant so after Ed

DID YOU KNOW . . . That the 1973 Bud Harrelson–Pete Rose fight had a little history to it? Harrelson had broken his hand when Cincinnati's Bill Plummer slid into him in June. Harrelson had also made disparaging remarks about Cincinnati's hitting early in the NLCS, and the Reds confronted him about it. So when Pete Rose went in hard on Harrelson in Game 3, Bud started one of the wildest fights Shea Stadium has ever seen. Harrelson lost the fight, the Mets took the pennant from the Reds, and the boos never stopped reigning on Rose in Flushing.

Kranepool informed the lefty he should apologize. The most memorable catchphrase in franchise history and the guy who coined it had to say he was sorry. That sums up M. Donald Grant—and Tug McGraw—perfectly.

The team started to play better, and the believing just fell in line. The Mets were mired in last place for most of the year, and Tug, who'd been in his worst slump since he'd mastered the screwball, caught fire. The Mets went from last place to first in five weeks in a weak division, and Tug was at the forefront. It was a time when relievers didn't have the developed roles they do now; they just pitched on a manager's hunch and whim. Tug came in as needed and stayed in until the game was over. He pitched a career-high 118 innings in 1973, averaging more than two innings per outing and starting twice as well. (Tug started 36 times for the Mets during his nine-year career in New York.) He even came to bat 24 times that year; by contrast, John Franco, who would shatter all Tug's (and later Jesse Orosco's) club records in the era of the "closer," only batted 15 times in 15 seasons as a Met.

Tug was on the hill when the Mets clinched the division title the day after the season was supposed to have ended. In the NLCS he got the last out and then ran like hell when the fans tore the field apart. He pitched five times covering 13⅔ innings in the World Series against Oakland (five more innings than starter Jerry Koosman logged), but Oakland outlasted New York in seven games. The Mets believed, but the A's knew.

The 1974 season was a bad one for the Mets and Tug. He started taking painkillers to numb his aching left shoulder, which sometimes left him unable to pick up the ball the day after appearances.

The club's solution was to make him a starter. They never looked into his arm trouble. Tug later said the Mets wanted to showcase him. With new general manager Joe McDonald taking over for retired Bob Scheffing, Tug told McDonald not to trade him to an American League team because of the designated hitter rule. (He really liked getting all those at-bats!) Tug was traded within the National League—to a division rival, no less—and the Mets thought they'd done well to get veteran center fielder Del Unser and promising catcher John Stearns, among others, for what they thought was damaged goods. The Phillies had no idea Tug had been hurting until he told them in spring training.

TRIVIA

Which two pitchers have started three games in a single World Series for the Mets?

Answers to the trivia questions are on pages 187–189.

Doctors found something inside his shoulder "about the size of a poached egg," he recalled. "It was a benign mass of gristle that had built up over the years. Removing it was a simple procedure. I was able to throw freely after that." And he threw well, too.

Tug debuted with Philadelphia in late April 1975, and he pitched another decade. He appeared in 16 postseason games with the Phillies and got the last six outs of the only world championship in that club's history. The Mets wrongly thought he was done. Relievers didn't last 19 years in the big leagues. This one did. He was special, all right.

Tug's free-spirited ways had consequences. In 1966, while playing for the Mets' minor league team in Jacksonville, he fathered a child with Betty D'Agostino. Tug, who soon married a stewardess he'd

By the NUMBERS **27**—Stolen bases by the 1973 pennant-winning club, the fewest ever by a Mets club over a full season (the 1994 club stole 25 in a strike-shortened 113 games). With an 82–79 record, the '73 Mets may have stolen the pennant, but they certainly didn't do it with speed. Wayne Garrett led the team with six thefts.

All-1970s Mets Team

Position	Name
First Baseman	John Milner
Second Baseman	Felix Millan
Shortstop	Bud Harrelson
Third Baseman	Wayne Garrett
Left Fielder	Dave Kingman
Center Fielder	Lee Mazzilli
Right Fielder	Rusty Staub
Catcher	John Stearns
Right-handed Pitcher	Tom Seaver
Left-handed Pitcher	Jerry Koosman
Relief Pitcher	Tug McGraw
Overlooked Pitcher	Craig Swan
Utility Player	Ed Kranepool
Manager	Yogi Berra

known for just a few months, denied responsibility for the child. Tug met the boy only twice during his playing career. He accepted Samuel Timothy McGraw as his son only after a lawsuit forced his hand. He helped Tim McGraw get his first recording contract and the man became country music royalty. After Tug was diagnosed with brain cancer in 2003, Tim McGraw remained at his side until the end. He and his wife, country star Faith Hill, paid for Tug's treatments and his care. Tug died in their Tennessee cabin on January 5, 2004. No one could ever stay mad at Tug; he was pure emotion, joy, and talent.

Tug always kept the game in perspective, a crucial attribute for someone playing a position where failure to hold a lead is greeted with the eagerness of a hernia. He played his whole career in New York and Philadelphia, where losing, though frequent, is not taken well. Tug's philosophy: "Ten million years from now, when the sun burns out and the earth is just a frozen ice ball hurtling through space, nobody's gonna care whether or not I got this guy out." But until the ice ball comes, the earth remains a more interesting place thanks to Tug McGraw.

Yogi Gotta Believe

The general impression of Yogi Berra is that of a smiling, genial man who can't help but say funny phrases wrapped with grains of hidden wisdom. Later generations that did not see him play may think of him as a comedian—the cartoon character Yogi Bear, after all, took its name from the catcher—but Yogi Berra, the ballplayer, won more pennants than any player in history. And with the addition of two rounds to the postseason format, it's unlikely anyone will ever approach the 14 World Series he appeared in.

The Yankees released the 38-year-old Yogi after the 1963 World Series and hired him as manager to succeed Ralph Houk, who took over as general manager. Yogi's slumping 1964 club was on its way out of Chicago following a sweep by the White Sox when reserve infielder Phil Linz started playing "Mary Had a Little Lamb" on his harmonica in the back of the bus. The ensuing confrontation became legend, and the Yankees rose from third place to the pennant, eventually losing to the Cardinals in an epic World Series. The Yankees made the unprecedented move of hiring the manager, Johnny Keane, who'd just beaten them. Yogi was out of the Yankees' organization for the first time since he'd signed with them in 1943. He found a new job, not far away, but in another world: the Mets.

Just as the Mets had relied on discarded Yankees heroes in manager Casey Stengel and team president George M. Weiss, the Mets offered a spot to the newly spurned Yankee. The Mets had two player/coaches in 1965, Berra and Warren Spahn. Berra played four games for the Mets in 1965, becoming the first former Most Valuable Player (a three-time MVP at that) to wear a Mets uniform. His job was to instruct—and boy, did they need it.

Stengel was still covering up the team's deficiencies with humor. After Danny Napoleon, the last man on the bench, won a game with an unlikely pinch-hit triple, Stengel strutted around the clubhouse singing "La Marseilles." Stengel broke his hip celebrating with his old cronies on the eve of his 75th birthday in July. Wes Westrum, another former New York catcher on the coaching staff, was named manager, and Yogi faded into the background, working with youngsters and occasionally entertaining the press with a new malapropism. He donned his Yankees uniform for Old Timer's Day at Shea (think that would happen now?) and celebrated with the '69 Mets. It was a comfortable new career for the man many still considered the best catcher of all time.

In 1973 Yogi Berra became the second manager to lead teams from both leagues to the World Series. Photo courtesy of Getty Images.

DID YOU KNOW . . . That a bizarre carom at Shea in 1973 played a major role in the miraculous Mets finish? After the Mets tied their September 20 game in the bottom of the ninth on Duffy Dyer's two-out double, it stayed tied into the top of the thirteenth. With two out, a drive by Pittsburgh's Dave Augustine hit the top of the wall in left and seemed sure to hop into the bullpen for a two-run homer. Defying physics, the ball bounced right to Cleon Jones, who relayed to shortstop Wayne Garrett, who fired to September call-up Ron Hodges, who tagged out Richie Zisk. Hodges singled home the winning run in the bottom of the inning. The Mets took over first place the next day.

Just days before the 1972 season was supposed to have started, manager Gil Hodges died of a massive heart attack after 27 holes of golf. Eddie Yost, Joe Pignatano, and Rube Walker, who witnessed their friend's death, would be Yogi's coaches in a matter of days.

Many felt the club was coldhearted in signing Yogi to a two-year contract before Hodges was even buried, especially since the season was to open late anyway because of a strike. The next day the club traded Tim Foli, Mike Jorgensen, and Ken Singleton to Montreal for Rusty Staub. The front office apparently dealt with grief by making deals.

Yogi gained the support of his veterans by playing a regular lineup, not the strict platoons of his predecessor. The Mets began the year at 8–2, which swelled to 25–7 after an 11-game winning streak. New York led Pittsburgh by six games in the NL East. Jon Matlack pitched a shutout on the next-to-last day of May to give him six straight wins to start his rookie year for the team with the best record in baseball. From there, the Mets were a 54–62 ballclub.

Although rookie slugger John Milner and Matlack, the eventual NL Rookie of the Year, provided more than the Mets could have hoped, the club's veterans faltered. New third baseman Jim Fregosi, for whom the team sacrificed Nolan Ryan, couldn't stay in the lineup. And when he wasn't hurt, he didn't hit. Tommie Agee's knees were in terrible shape. Staub injured his hand. Cleon Jones hurt his elbow playing first base. Elbow chips limited Jerry Grote to just 64 games. Willie Mays, picked up in May from the Giants amid deafening

IF ONLY . . . The Mets had scored an extra run or two at the right time in the 1973 World Series. The Mets lost the opener, 2–1, dropped Game 3 in 11 innings at Shea, 3–2, and fell with Tom Seaver on the hill and a chance to clinch in six games, 3–1. Dozens of things had fallen into place as the Mets went from last place in August to first place with a scant 82 wins; if another bloop had fallen in against Oakland, the second Mets miracle might have been complete. The Mets outscored the Swingin' A's, 24–21.

applause, had great moments but showed creakiness in his 41-year-old body. New York finished 13½ games behind the Pirates.

Nothing seemed to go right for the club for most of 1973. Matlack was literally knocked out of a game on May 8 by a line drive. He wound up in the intensive care unit with a hairline skull fracture, and his 3–1 lead turned into a loss when the ball caromed off his head into the Mets dugout to spark an Atlanta rally. His catcher, Jerry Grote, had his forearm snapped by a pitch by Pittsburgh's Ramon Hernandez. Seven Mets went on the disabled list, the team ebbed, and the bullpen couldn't make up for the injuries. Everyone from Willie Mays to Tug McGraw voiced their displeasure. The second-guessers had Yogi pegged as the scapegoat.

Team president M. Donald Grant's speech was interrupted by McGraw's rallying cry, "Ya Gotta Believe," which soon reached every corner of the city. People believed, and the team played better as the injured players came back, but the biggest boost was playing in a division of middling teams. On August 14 the Mets were 13 games under .500 and in last place in the National League East, yet they were only eight and a half games out; they would have been almost 20 games back in the NL West. From that point on, the Mets went 30–14.

With 21 games to go, Yogi announced the Mets would go to a four-man rotation: Tom Seaver, Jerry Koosman, Matlack, and George Stone. It worked. By September 16, with Grote and McGraw lighting it up, the Mets, though still in fourth place, stood just two and a half games out of first. A scheduling quirk had the Mets and the division-leading Pirates playing five consecutive games between Three Rivers Stadium and Shea. Pittsburgh won the first game, but the Mets took the next four. On September 21 the Mets were in first place by three percentage points with a .500 record and eight games to go.

The Mets won their next three, giving them seven straight wins and a one-and-a-half-game lead. The Mets lost their final home game to Montreal, and then went to Chicago, where it did nothing but rain. The Pirates dropped three straight games and fell to third as the Cardinals flew into second. The Mets, meanwhile, waited in a soggy clubhouse at Wrigley Field. New York split a doubleheader the final Sunday of the year and had to play another twin bill the next afternoon to decide the race once and for all. In front of just 1,913 fans at Wrigley, Rick Monday's two-run homer in the seventh sent Yogi to get Seaver and bring in McGraw. He retired all but one batter he faced over three innings, and that base runner was erased when Glenn Beckert, batting for Monday, hit a line drive to Milner, who stepped on the base for a double play and the club's second division title. This one, believe it or not, was more unlikely than their first.

The National League Championship Series went the distance but was only hard-fought near second base at Shea Stadium. With the series tied and the Mets hammering the Reds in Game 3, Pete Rose hammered back. No players were ejected in the mêlée, but when Rose went out to his position in left field in the bottom of the inning, he was pelted with debris. Yogi led a contingent that included Seaver, Mays, Staub, and Jones to plead with the fans to stop. Rose came back out amid boos that never relented during his final 13 years as a visiting player. Although Rose's homer won the game the next day, the Mets won the pennant handily behind Seaver in Game 5.

Yogi was the second to manage in a World Series in each league (Joe McCarthy was the first), with both of his pennants coming as a result of stirring September comebacks. Like his 1964 flag with the Yankees, this one ended sadly. Despite the lowest winning percentage (.509) for a team in World Series history, the Mets outhit, outscored, and outpitched the A's in the Series. New York took a three-games-to-two lead before dropping the last two games in Oakland. No other expansion team had ever finished a season in first place, much less won two pennants.

TOP 10

Yogi Berra Boo-Boos at Shea (1965–1975)

1. "It ain't over 'til it's over."—When no one believed, July 1973.
2. "If you ain't got a bullpen, you ain't got nothin'."— Midway through 1973 season.
3. "Tony Perez is a big clog in their machine."—Speaking about Cincinnati's Big Red Machine, October 1973.
4. "You don't look so hot yourself."—Reply to Mary Lindsay, who commented how cool Yogi looked after her husband, Mayor John Lindsay, gave Yogi the key to the city on a hot, humid day.
5. "If you can't imitate him, don't copy him."—As a coach to Ron Swoboda, who was trying to bat like Frank Robinson in batting practice.
6. "I don't know if we're the oldest battery, but we're certainly the ugliest."—On catching ancient (and ordinary-looking) Warren Spahn in one of Yogi's four games playing for the Mets in 1965.
7. "We're lost, but we're making good time!"—On the way to Cooperstown with his family for his Hall of Fame induction in August 1972.
8. "You give us Jonesy and Rusty and Milner playing a full season and hitting the way they can, I'll take my chances. I won't need another hitter if they play every day."—Before the Mets tumbled to fifth place in 1974.
9. "We were overwhelming underdogs."—Reminiscing with Nolan Ryan about the 1969 Mets.
10. "Good players."—When asked what makes a good manager.

But 1974 was a letdown. Even as the Mets tumbled, fans thought the team could come back as they'd done twice in five seasons. As it became apparent that neither the Mets nor the runaway Pirates would allow this to happen, the heat turned on Yogi. A Banner Day greeting of "Impeach Yogi"—mirroring President Nixon's tumultuous summer—was a sign of things to come.

Injuries continued to plague the team in 1975. Yogi went with a three-man rotation early in the season to take advantage of the few able bodies and the many holes in the schedule. The Mets did not score for 35 consecutive innings at Shea, which was now, with the Yankees playing there for the second straight year, the center of New York's baseball universe.

Yogi's biggest problem, though, was in Florida, where Cleon Jones recovered from knee surgery. Local authorities caught the married Jones in a compromising situation with a young woman in a van. Jones was forced to make a public apology to his teammates with his wife by his side, and he then sat the bench at Shea after his knee healed. He refused to take the field as a substitute in a July 18 game, argued with Yogi, and left the stadium.

The manager demanded that Jones be suspended for insubordination. Jones refused a trade to the Angels and, despite an apology to the manager, was given his unconditional release. Yogi had won the battle, but he had lost the backing of the front office and many of his players. When the last-place Expos blanked the Mets twice in one day in August, Yogi was replaced by Coach Roy McMillan. The egomaniacal Grant said he'd wanted to dump Yogi since 1973. So much for "Ya Gotta Believe."

Bad Moves Risin'

The founding of the Mets was the achievement of a hard-fought goal of bringing National League baseball back to New York. The organization had the same goal every professional sports team has: to win a championship. It was more of a dream than an actual business plan, but after the Mets shocked every man, woman, and child in the country by taking the 1969 World Series, they were faced with a legitimate question they had never dared considered: What now?

What, indeed. The club took a look at its organizational needs and the one clear, crying necessity was for hitting. Third base was an obvious starting point. The team's desperation at third base was illustrated in the platoon at the hot corner for the 1969 club. Left-handed hitter Wayne Garrett, 21, was the youngest player on the team; right-swinging Ed Charles, 36, was the oldest. Together they combined to hit .214 with an on-base percentages below .300. Defensively, they combined for 15 errors and 19 double plays. Like everything else for the 1969 Mets, the arrangement somehow worked. Charles glided into retirement after the world championship, and the Mets set their sights on finding a new man for the hot corner. How abysmal was this third-base search? Garrett, who only got slightly better as a hitter, wound up playing the majority of the time at the position for the Mets until 1976. In the meantime, the Mets gave up two of the best players they ever produced at two positions.

The first sacrificial lamb in the search for a third baseman was Amos Otis. Otis was only 22 and he batted just .151 in 93 at-bats in 1969. When he'd come up at age 20, he'd hit somewhat better. Although the Mets tried unsuccessfully to make him a third baseman, Otis was a superb outfielder. He never made an error in 51 career games in New York's outfield and he added five assists. And he was from Mobile, Alabama, the same hometown as left fielder Cleon Jones and center fielder Tommie Agee. Time would soon tell that Otis was the best of the bunch.

Joe Foy was the third baseman on the "Impossible Dream" Red Sox pennant-winner in 1967. A year later he was taken by the Royals in the expansion draft. That a 25-year-old third baseman with speed and power was left unprotected should have set off bells for a team looking to deal for him, but a rebound year in Kansas City masked Foy's declining fortunes. So Otis became a Royal. They also held out for top Mets pitching prospect Bob Johnson. Johnson wasn't too special, but Kansas City was able to flip him to Pittsburgh a year later to bring over little but lion-hearted shortstop Fred Patek, giving the

"How long can you wait?" was the Mets' explanation for trading inconsistent 24-year-old Nolan Ryan. Apparently, not long enough.

Royals two cornerstone players for their eventual domination of the American League West.

By 1970 Foy's personal problems and poor play resulted in him being left unprotected again. (The Washington Senators took him.) By then, just a year after the trade, Otis was already an All-Star center fielder, embarking on a career in Kansas City (2,020 hits, 1,007 RBIs, 341 steals, three Gold Gloves) that no Mets center fielder—or everyday player, for that matter—has ever approached.

Still, it's difficult to hold it against general manager Johnny Murphy. He engineered the final personnel moves that helped make the Mets world champions in 1969, and he died of a heart attack just a month after the Otis deal. His successor, Bob Scheffing, gets no such pass.

The new Mets third baseman in 1971, Bob Aspromonte, had only cost Ron Herbel in a trade with Atlanta. The Aspromonte experiment (.225 average, 15 double plays grounded into, 10 double plays turned) had Scheffing looking elsewhere after the season. Again, they had a player they weren't sure what to do with, a hard-throwing but wild right-hander: Nolan Ryan.

TRIVIA

Who was the first Met to score more than 100 runs in a season?

Answers to the trivia questions are on pages 187–189.

Ryan had been with the Mets off and on since 1966, and in 1971 he enjoyed his best season as a regular in the rotation. His 10 wins were more than Jerry Koosman or Ray Sadecki had, and while his 137–116 strikeout-to-walk ratio was alarming (figure in 15 hit batters and six wild pitches), he was making strides. Pitching coach Rube Walker and experience were slowly taming the wild colt, but Scheffing long deflected blame for the trade on Ryan himself and on Ryan's wife, Ruth, whose name would later be used as the final straw for trading Tom Seaver in 1977.

Scheffing said Ruth Ryan didn't like living in New York and wanted to go somewhere less hectic. Scheffing also said Ryan threatened to retire if he wasn't traded. That, to put it nicely, is crap. There was no free agency or leverage for a player at the time, and the idea that someone who could throw as hard as Ryan simply quitting at age 24 sounds like a bluff. And it's not like Ryan was traded to sleepy

The Mets had chosen Whitey Herzog to succeed Johnny Murphy as general manager in 1970. With no second-in-command in place after Murphy's sudden passing, team chairman M. Donald Grant practically dragged top scout Bob Scheffing from his Arizona home to run the club. As longtime Mets beat man Jack Lang opined, "No one knew the organization better than Whitey. But Herzog was too strong-minded and too opinionated for Grant's tastes. He had frequently told the Mets' chairman of the board in organizational meetings that he should let baseball men make baseball decisions."

Milwaukee or to the Rangers, who'd just relocated, or dealt to Houston, near his hometown of Alvin. Scheffing sent Ryan to the Angels, who played so close to Los Angeles they've since switched their name to make it so. L.A. is no small burg.

"We've had him three full years and, although he's a hell of a prospect, he hasn't done it for us," Scheffing said when the trade was made. "How long can you wait? I can't rate him in the same category with Tom Seaver, Jerry Koosman, or Gary Gentry." On the other end of the phone, Angels general manager Harry Dalton said Ryan had "the best arm in the National League and at 24, he's just coming into his own." This came from the man who, as a first-year general manager in Baltimore, stole Frank Robinson from Cincinnati after the 1965 season.

Always willing to overpay with young players, Scheffing threw the Angels three other prospects for New York's new third baseman, who'd never played third base before. Jim Fregosi, an original Angel and a six-time All-Star shortstop, was coming off his worst year as a regular, enduring a sore arm, a strained muscle in his side, and a tumor on his foot. He had just five homers, 33 RBIs, and a .233 average in '71; he produced slightly less for the Mets in '72, with a like number of maladies. Ryan won 19 games his first year as an Angel, made the All-Star team, and struck out 329 batters, the most in the American League in 26 years. The next season Ryan started throwing no-hitters.

Mets manager Gil Hodges agreed with the Ryan trade as a "now" deal, but predicted, "He could put things together overnight." Hodges never saw Ryan pitch in the AL or Fregosi play third base at

Worst Mets Trades

1. **Nolan Ryan** to the Angels, December 10, 1971: Their fruitless quest for a third baseman led to this. They even sent the Angels three more prospects for past-his-prime Jim Fregosi, who'd never played third base before and failed to hit in the National League.

2. **Amos Otis** to the Royals, December 3, 1969: Trading this blue chip for third base failure Joe Foy led to the Ryan-for-Fregosi debacle two years later.

3. **Tom Seaver** to the Reds, June 15, 1977: Oh, the humanity. Whichever order you place Pat Zachry, Dan Norman, Steve Henderson, and Doug Flynn in, it still comes up to a hill of beans.

4. **Rusty Staub** to the Tigers, December 12, 1975: They already had one of the league's elite rotations, yet they traded their best hitter for a pitcher, Mickey Lolich, who quit after one lousy year at Shea. The Mets had dealt three good young players—including Ken Singleton—to Montreal to get Staub in 1972.

5. **Len Dykstra** to the Phillies, June 18, 1989: However he did it, Dykstra led the Phils to the World Series the year the Mets lost 103 games. Throw-in Roger McDowell had several good years left, too. Juan Samuel played exactly 86 games and hit .228 as a Met. Frank Cashen's worst deal.

6. **Scott Kazmir** to the Devil Rays, July 30, 2004: Look for this one to rise on the chart as Victor Zambrano's New York career tanked and Kazmir became an All-Star at 22.

7. **Jason Isringhausen** to the A's, July 31, 1999: How'd this call go? "Let's see, how about we give you an up-and-coming former wunderkind who we've waited on for four years because he has such a good arm and you give us whatever you have lying around. Oh, and we'll throw in a reliever we've traded for twice [Greg McMichael]." Done. Billy Taylor had an 8.10 ERA as a Met and was rightfully left off the postseason roster.

8. **Jeff Reardon** to the Expos, May 29, 1981: A hard-throwing reliever (plus Dan Norman) for a once-solid outfielder coming off being hit in the face. Ellis Valentine never strode into a pitch again and was actually worse than the lousy outfielders the Mets already had. It was so bad the Angels later tried to make the strong-armed Valentine a pitcher. Reardon went on to briefly hold the all-time save record and earned the last out in Minnesota's 1987 world championship.

9. **Jeff Kent** to the Indians, July 29, 1996: Kent and Jose Vizcaino went to Cleveland for Alvaro Espinoza, who played 48 games as a Met, and Carlos Baerga, a slugging second baseman with an outside shot at the Hall of Fame. Things changed quickly. Kent became the masher mentioned with Rogers Hornsby while Baerga didn't even measure up to Vizcaino as a Met. As with the Jason Bay deal in 2002, a future superstar was soon dealt again: Kent (and Vizcaino) went to San Francisco for Matt Williams.

10. **Melvin Mora** to the Orioles, July 28, 2000: The Mets didn't think they could get to the World Series with a defensively shaky shortstop (Mora had replaced injured Rey Ordoñez). New York's pop-gun outfield sure could have used the beloved Mora. Veteran shortstop Mike Bordick didn't make many errors or get many hits. He was hurt during the 2000 World Series and immediately returned to the Orioles as a free agent. Mora's done fine in Baltimore, too.

Shea; the Mets manager died of a heart attack shortly before the '72 season began.

In the midst of the shock of his passing, the elevation of Yogi Berra to manager, Hodges's funeral, and the canceling of Opening Day in the first strike in major league history, Scheffing made another big trade in search of offense. Rusty Staub, an idol in Montreal, was procured from Parc Jarry for three top prospects: shortstop Tim Foli, first baseman Mike Jorgensen, and outfielder Ken Singleton. Foli and Jorgensen became everyday major leaguers, while Singleton emerged as a star in Baltimore after the Expos dealt him with Mike Torrez for Dave McNally and Rich Coggins in a trade almost the equal to the doozies coming out of New York.

Staub, however, was a difference maker, bringing the Mets a potent lefty bat in the middle of the order. On May 11, 1972, Scheffing bought a present for owner Joan Payson, a longtime New York Giants fan and stockholder. Willie Mays returned to New York for reliever Charlie Williams and $50,000. Even with his long and glorious career running on fumes, Mays homered in his first game as a Met—against the Giants, no less—and he generated much good press while Otis and Ryan were highlighting the papers' out-of-town coverage.

Scheffing pulled off one of his best deals after the 1972 season, getting second baseman Felix Millan and southpaw George Stone from the Braves for fading Gary Gentry and star-crossed Danny Frisella. Stone and Millan were key parts of the Mets' 1973 plan: "How to win a pennant in six weeks without really trying." Scheffing then dealt aging Agee to Houston for two prospects who didn't pan out, leaving the team without a center fielder. The Mets plugged in light-hitting Don Hahn, whom Scheffing had acquired from Montreal for Ron Swoboda in 1971.

Lee Mazzilli was Scheffing's only first-round draft pick even remotely of note. Meanwhile, his deals shipped out scores of talented young players uncovered by director of personnel Whitey Herzog, who fell out of favor with club president M. Donald Grant and ran away to become manager in Texas. Herzog later worked wonders in Kansas City and St. Louis.

While Scheffing's trades dug a huge hole for the club, successor Joe McDonald's moves were like filling a grave with dirt. He traded the club's top reliever and its heart and soul, Tug McGraw, to a division rival. While John Stearns went on to have a solid Mets career and Del Unser looked good in center field for a season and a half—until another bad deal sent Unser and Garrett to Montreal—McGraw took his screwball and enthusiasm (not to mention his screwball enthusiasm) to a Philadelphia team that was shaking off a decade of dormancy and building toward a power.

McDonald was able to move on the go, picking up reliever Skip Lockwood, buying unwanted slugger Dave Kingman for $150,000, getting shortstop Mike Phillips as Bud Harrelson continued his brittle period, and acquiring phenom/flash-in-the-pan outfielder Mike Vail. It was Vail's astonishing 23-game hitting streak after his August 1975 debut that made McDonald think that Staub, the first 100-RBI man in Mets history, was expendable. So Staub went to Detroit for Mickey Lolich, the hero of the 1968 World Series and the all-time southpaw strikeout king at the time. Vail almost simultaneously blew out his ankle playing pickup basketball and went on to a mediocre career. Lolich took to New York about as well as Nolan Ryan's wife; he retired after a year.

The 1976 season was a mirage. Rookie manager Joe Frazier, McDonald's choice, used steely eyed determination to lead the way, backed by Kingman home runs and Koosman wins. Tom Seaver? His only problem was run support. Right.

It was all window dressing, a pleasant-looking house rotting from within. And it all came crashing down.

Grant's Tomb

The Mets' descent into hell began as a seemingly pleasant journey. Dave Kingman, who, in his first year with the club, 1975, had become the first Met to hit 30 home runs since 1962, launched home runs in 1976 at a rate and distance that no one at Shea had ever imagined. Kong, with 30 home runs by July 10, was the first Met voted to start the All-Star Game since Willie Mays in 1972. Tom Seaver, fresh off becoming the first right-hander to win three Cy Young Awards, was also an All-Star along with Jon Matlack, who'd earned the win and co-MVP in the previous year's midsummer classic. Although the Mets went into the break four games over .500, they were a mile behind the Phillies, who'd traded in their doormat status of the past decade. The Mets were light years behind the Yankees, who'd reopened Yankee Stadium, taken over the American League East, and attracted huge crowds to the Bronx after two years as guests at Shea Stadium.

Still, by Mets standards, the 1976 season was going all right under rookie manager Joe Frazier. Then Phil Niekro hit a fly ball to left field in the third inning on July 19. Kingman, a brutal fielder to begin with, tore a thumb ligament diving for the ball. His 32 home runs in 87 games had given him a remote chance to break the single-season home run mark, but after missing six weeks, he wouldn't even win the NL home run title.

Although the Mets remained over .500—and their 86 wins represented the second-highest total in club history—not even Jerry Koosman's pursuit of 20 wins (he made it) and a possible Cy Young Award (he finished second) brought much enthusiasm to Shea while the reconstructed Yankee Stadium and that face-lifted franchise beckoned those fans whose memories of 1969 and 1973 had started to dim. And M. Donald Grant certainly wasn't helping.

The death of matriarch Joan Payson—coming less than a week after Casey Stengel's passing in the fall of 1975—signaled a change to a more parsimonious front office. With the coming of full-fledged free agency, the subject of money filtered into the sports pages. The news was not good for the Mets. Tom Seaver angered Grant by asking for $275,000 annually over three years in 1976. It led to a Seaver-for-Don Sutton trade proposal that never came to pass. The Mets worked out a three-year contract with Seaver that featured the first written incentives requiring league approval. In retrospect, the trade to the Dodgers would have been far better than what actually happened.

Seaver's relationship with the club wasn't the only one that was deteriorating. Several Mets were irked that the Mets failed to sign any players in the first-ever free agent draft in November 1976. In a system that required interested teams to draft free agents and then

Pat Zachry was one of the rotation's mainstays during the lean late 1970s. Photo courtesy of Getty Images.

try to woo them, the Mets timidly pursued the eight players they expressed interest in. Matlack said the team lied to him about upgrading personnel. Surly Kingman joined in, demanding a trade and saying he would become a free agent after the '77 season.

By the end of May, 1977, the Mets were 13 games out, and Manager Joe Frazier was replaced by infielder Joe Torre, who, in October 1974, had been the first player Mets general manager Joe McDonald ever traded for. The Mets went 11–5, with Torre briefly serving as the only player/manager in franchise history. As the trade deadline approached, dark clouds gathered over Shea Stadium, but it still could have worked out.

Seaver reconciled with management, going over Grant's head to owner Linda de Roulet, Joan Payson's daughter, and working out the basis of a two-year contract extension worth $700,000 that would have kept him in New York through 1980. Seaver was sitting poolside in Atlanta the day of the trading deadline when he heard about a *New York Daily News* column by Dick Young, whose son-in-law worked for Grant and the Mets. It read, "Nolan Ryan is getting more money than Tom Seaver, and that galls Tom because Nancy Seaver and Ruth Ryan are very friendly and Tom Seaver has long treated Nolan Ryan like a little brother." Seaver changed his mind, got on the phone, scotched the deal with the Mets, and demanded a trade. He had earlier received permission to talk to two-time defending world champion Cincinnati, and that was where he was sent for four young players. Only in a world where free agency was new could a New York team send its star *to* Cincinnati and get prospects in return.

Seaver cried, fans cried, and people in New York who previously couldn't imagine their lives without the Mets started living just fine without them. That same night Kingman was traded to San Diego for Bobby Valentine, a one-time star prospect turned utility player by

By the NUMBERS **2.43**—ERA by Craig Swan in 1978 to lead the National League for the last-place Mets. Swan had just a 9–6 record with 13 no-decisions for the offensively challenged club. It marked the only time a Met led the league in ERA between Tom Seaver in 1973 and Dwight Gooden in 1985.

DID YOU KNOW . . . That the Mets had a mule as a mascot in 1979 called Mettle? (As if being a Mets fans in the late 1970s wasn't embarrassing enough.)

injury, and lefty reliever Paul Siebert. (Those hearing the news on crackling radios hoped momentarily they'd gotten Seaver back, but no, it was just Siebert.) Mike Phillips was sent to St. Louis for Joel Youngblood in what turned out to be a good trade, but the deals, culminated in the closing minutes of the June 15 trade deadline, would go down as the "Midnight Massacre." Shea Stadium became irrelevant. Kingman's ominous words, "I hate to think how lousy they're going to be in a couple of years," proved to be way ahead of schedule.

If only that's where the story ended. The delusion of years of .500 clubs just a couple of players away cracked wide open. This team was awful, and not in any way like the fumbling, cuddly Mets of Marvelous Marv. The Mets staggered and sputtered through the rest of the 1970s like a stricken man knocking things over in his final moments before finally hitting the floor, dead. The Mets had a long, agonizing death scene. They were exactly 100 games below .500 (193–293) between 1977 and 1979.

Jerry Grote appeared in the 1977 World Series in New York...at Yankee Stadium as a member of the Dodgers. The former catching great, now a backup, had been traded to L.A. for cash and two minor leaguers at the end of August. Jon Matlack and John Milner were next to go. They were sent away in a four-team trade that netted flamboyant first baseman Willie Montanez. Like Lenny Randle the previous year, Montanez brought some life to the corpse. His stutter-step home run trot and snap catches were fun to watch in 1978, but it was just a sideshow to a lousy main event.

The Mets signed their first free agent, minor leaguer Tom Hausman, and then inked Elliott Maddox, whose knee had been ruined playing at Shea Stadium while with the Yankees. The Mets bought feisty old pal Tim Foli to play shortstop, precipitating the trading of erstwhile shortstop Bud Harrelson to Philadelphia in spring training. Left fielder Steve Henderson made strides while hustling John Stearns set a record for the most stolen bases in a season

"MIDNIGHT" MASSACRE" EPILOGUE

Here's how the players traded for each other in the Mets-Reds deal of June 15, 1977, fared during their careers in their new homes.

Pat Zachry: 41–46 as a Met with a 3.63 ERA in six seasons in New York. No 200-inning seasons, but named an All-Star in 1978.

Doug Flynn: .234 batting average, .264 on-base percentage, .292 slugging percentage in five seasons, with five home runs and 155 RBIs as a Met; one Gold Glove. Once deemed "untouchable" by a delusional Joe Torre, he was peddled to Texas shortly after Torre's firing in 1981.

Steve Henderson: The jewel of Cincinnati's farm system and the supposed key to the Seaver deal, he hit .287 with a .360 on-base percentage and .423 slugging percentage over four years. He was sent to the Cubs with cash for Dave Kingman, who had been traded by the Mets the same night as Seaver.

Dan Norman: Billed as a great talent, Norman couldn't even break into the Mets' punchless outfield. He had 100 bats in just one of four seasons, and he failed in his attempt to switch hit.

Tom Seaver: He did just fine in Cincinnati. Although the Reds only made the playoffs once in his five-plus seasons there, he threw his only career no-hitter in 1978, was the best pitcher of the 1981 strike season (although "Fernandomania" robbed him of his fourth Cy Young), and was 75–46, with a 3.18 ERA, in 158 starts for Cincy. Three seasons after the old regime ended—and Seaver's numbers started to decline—New York got him back, trading three supposedly promising players to the Reds for the return of their franchise pitcher.

for a catcher. Pat Zachry won 10 games by the All-Star break but broke his foot kicking the dugout step after allowing a Pete Rose single that extended his hitting streak to 37 consecutive games, tying the modern National League record. Seaver watched from the other dugout. Zachry was out for the year; so were the Mets.

The 1979 season seemed to last a decade. Competing for the entertainment dollar against the two-time defending world champion Yankees, the Mets drew under one million fans for the first time at Shea Stadium. They acquired former Pirates Frank Taveras, Richie

Hebner, and Dock Ellis in separate deals to little effect, while Foli, sent to Pittsburgh, wound up winning a World Series as their everyday shortstop. Lee Mazzilli, shoved down the fans' throats as the only remotely marketable player, homered to tie the All-Star Game and brought in the winning run with a bases-loaded walk, but Pirate Dave Parker took MVP honors because of a great throw. The Mets snoozed until late September, losing 15 of 17 games to sit at 57–99. Somehow, the Mets reeled off six straight wins to avoid their first 100-loss season since 1967.

The same year that the last original Met, Ed Kranepool, played his final game, the family that had owned the Mets since day one announced it was selling the team. Linda de Roulet had replaced M. Donald Grant as president before the 1979 season, but she was even less effective than the loathed Grant. Meanwhile, her father's financial devotion to this baseball venture was at its end. Although de Roulet tried, and she certainly was thrifty, the franchise as presently constituted would not make money. After years of sinking, the Mets had finally hit bottom; they needed someone willing to go all the way down and pull them back up.

TRIVIA

Which future Mets manager did Tom Seaver retire to end his last game as a Met before the calamitous trade of June 15, 1977?

Answers to the trivia questions are on pages 187–189.

Coming Soon: Hope

The new owners had their work cut out for them. What they bought wasn't worth much and they paid dearly for one reason: the Mets stationery said "New York." The Doubleday publishing fortune put up 80 percent of the record purchase price of $21.1 million, securing a team that had been run into the ground and a lease at a stadium where the bloom was off the rose.

Fred Wilpon ran the show from the start. He'd partnered with Nelson Doubleday to supply the capital to buy the club and brought Sandy Koufax to the initial press conference to tell the world for the first time—but not the last—about a man who was such a good high school pitcher in Brooklyn that Koufax spent most of his time playing first base.

The new era began on a Thursday, April 10, against the Cubs. The Mets won, 5–2, in front of 12,219. Three other dates on the 3–3 home stand added together did not even equal that modest Opening Day attendance figure. Then the Mets traveled to Wrigley Field and were promptly swept by what would be the worst Cubs team in 15 seasons. It didn't feel very new.

But the Mets tried different things to spruce up the 16-year-old ballpark that looked twice its age. While Shea hosted its first Grucci Brothers Fireworks Night and Wilpon touched heaven with a salute to the 1955 Brooklyn Dodgers, there was also a Twinkie Night doubleheader and a softball game featuring Playboy bunnies to benefit Lighthouse for the Blind. Although Jacket Night was so successful they ran out of jackets, it was offset by the decision to replace a large section of upper deck seats on Father's Day weekend. The Mets, coming off a five-run ninth to stun the Giants on Saturday night,

IF ONLY . . . The Mets hadn't lost Tom Seaver twice. The first time, they famously traded him to Cincinnati in 1977, but the second time he was left unprotected in the free agent compensation pool in place at the time and was snatched by the White Sox after his 1983 comeback with the Mets. He won his 300th game for Chicago in 1985 and missed being elder statesman on the same staff as Dwight Gooden, Ron Darling, and Sid Fernandez

turned away thousands of fathers and sons the next day on what was the biggest crowd in two years. For the season, however, attendance increased by 400,000.

On July 17 the Mets were actually at .500 following a victory by John Pacella, best known for his hat flying off after every pitch. The Mets were just four and a half games out of first in a tight NL East race. The brief, giddy adventure with the first division—and .500—didn't last. The Mets dropped like a stone and lost 95 times, a number they reached in each of Joe Torre's first four seasons at the helm. The Mets would not hit that figure in 1981, but many factors conspired to test new ownership's patience.

General manager Frank Cashen, who'd built Baltimore into a powerhouse in the late 1960s and early 1970s, had made one remotely significant move his maiden New York year in 1980. He traded for Claudell Washington in June and then watched him sign with Atlanta as a free agent in November. Cashen, called "Bowtie" for his favored neckwear, was much busier in year two.

The Mets acquired infielder Bob Bailor, whom Cashen's Orioles had signed as a high schooler in 1969. The GM signed free agents Randy Jones and Mike Cubbage. Cashen's two biggest moves involved old Mets Rusty Staub and Dave Kingman. Staub had settled in as a designated hitter type—and his size had grown with the role—while Kingman was the long-ball threat the Mets desperately needed. (Despite missing half Chicago's games in 1980, Kingman still hit more home runs than any Met.) Kingman cost New York Steve Henderson, but the Mets had gotten as much out of Hendu as there was to be gotten.

All these changes were cosmetic. The Mets weren't going to realistically contend, but Cashen inadvertently helped Montreal reach the postseason for the only time in its history by sending reliever Jeff Reardon (and Dan Norman) across the border for Ellis Valentine. It was one of Cashen's worst moves. Reardon not only led the National League in fewest runners per nine innings and had a 1.30 ERA for *les Expos* in 1981, but he went on to briefly hold the all-time saves record. Just 10 of his 367 saves came with the team that signed the undrafted University of Massachusetts pitcher the day before the "Midnight Massacre" of 1977. Valentine had been hit in the face in 1980, and his fearsome power stroke was gone. The gun-shy right fielder with a gun for an arm hit just 13 home runs in 159 games as a Met. Neil Allen's dependability in late innings made the 25-year-old Reardon available, but Allen blew nine saves and didn't help his manager's tenuous position; the strike helped even less.

TRIVIA

The Mets set the record for most singles the same year they established a mark for fewest home runs over a full schedule. What year was it?

Answers to the trivia questions are on pages 187–189.

After Tom Seaver beat the Mets to complete a Cincinnati sweep June 11, Shea Stadium and all of baseball went dark for two months. When the lights came back on, the 17–34 Mets had a clean slate—the split season gave the club a reprieve—and the Mets won the first three games after the strike. The mirage of a division chase lasted longer than usual, but it ended just the same.

The season was utterly forgettable save for the emergence of rookies Hubie Brooks and Mookie Wilson. Injuries in the first half cost the club Craig Swan and former UCLA standout Tim Leary (Torre had pushed to have Leary, the 1979 second overall pick, on the staff; Leary left his major league debut after two innings and did not pitch for the Mets again for two years.) Randy Jones and Tom Hausman were both injured in an exhibition game in Toronto just after the strike was settled. No Met won more than seven times, and the 41 victories (in 105 games) was just one more than the "Metaclysmic" 1962 squad. Torre was let go the last Sunday of the season.

George Bamberger was the only person Cashen wanted to take over the club. Bamberger had been pitching coach under Earl Weaver with all those magnificent O's pitchers. He took over perennially drab

Dave Kingman's 37 home runs in 1982 led the National League, but his .204 average was equally conspicuous. Photo courtesy of Getty Images.

8—Consecutive pinch hits by Rusty Staub in 1983. His ninth-inning single on June 26 against Philadelphia's Ron Reed tied the mark set by pinch hitter Dave Philley of the 1958 Phillies. The 39-year-old Staub finished the season with a record 81 at-bats as a pinch hitter, and fell one shy of another record with 24 pinch hits.

Milwaukee in 1978, and the club transformed into "Bambi's Bombers." A heart attack forced him to quit managing in 1980. He had no inkling to manage again, yet he was easily persuaded.

"What the heck, Frank is an old friend," Bamberger said. "He needed me. I couldn't let him down. I did it for Frank, no other reason." Frankly, the next two years were a disaster.

The 1982 club featured the most unusual of luxuries at Shea Stadium: two sluggers in the same lineup. George Foster had been brought over at great expense—something that never would have happened under M. Donald Grant—but he left his productivity in Cincinnati. Foster hit just 13 home runs and drove in 70 in 151 games, his lowest output in either category since 1974. Dave Kingman hit 37 homers—the first time a Met led the NL in any major offensive category—and he knocked in 99. Still, Kingman batted .204, whiffed 156 times, and committed 18 errors. Same old Kong. Same old Mets. They lost 97 games. Torre, meanwhile, took the Braves to their first divisional title since 1969.

At the winter meetings in Honolulu, Cashen put together the most emotionally significant deal by the club since Willie Mays came over from the Giants a decade earlier. The Mets put the Franchise back in the franchise as Tom Seaver ended five years in exile. The Reds felt Seaver was done, but coming back to New York gave Tom Terrific a career jolt, even if his 9–14 record with the Mets didn't show it. Seaver also jolted fans awake, even if it was just for a day.

April 5 was a spectacular Tuesday afternoon with warm sunshine that invited hooky. Walking through the concourse and seeing the blue sky and green grass was like awakening after a long slumber. Eight other Mets starters were on the field while the pitching mound remained empty. As the noise steadily built from the 48,000 on hand, PA announcer Jack Franchetti beamed: "And pitching, number 41..."

No name needed. The ovation lasted five minutes, Seaver lasted six innings, and Doug Sisk earned his first major league win in relief, a 2–0 triumph over the Phillies.

That was pretty much the season. After that one glorious afternoon the first week of April, the rest of 1983, in retrospect, seemed like cocktail hour before a big event. George Bamberger had to leave suddenly. Mister Neil Allen and Master Rick Ownbey departed quickly, too. In their place came an agitated Keith Hernandez, but he managed to settle down and actually started enjoying himself. Darryl Strawberry got there early amid much chatter and managed to have a good time. Dave Kingman sulked in the corner, George Foster sat quietly, and Rusty Staub was busy in the kitchen. Jesse Orosco? He'd been there all along. He was waiting and waiting to get inside and see what kind of a shindig this was going to be. After all, this was New York. Wasn't it?

Managing a Turnaround

Davey Johnson took a most circuitous route from one Mets world championship to the next. As second baseman for the Orioles, Johnson made the last out at Shea Stadium to end Game 5 as the Mets won the 1969 World Series. Then he ran for safety in the bedlam that followed. In 1986 he stood in the dugout, watching the last pitch. Then he rushed into the mob to join in the mayhem at Shea Stadium.

Johnson had a long and distinguished career as a player. He was a three-time All-Star and Gold Glove winner at second base for the Orioles until he was traded to Atlanta to make room for Bobby Grich. He was a part of the first trio to ever hit 40 home runs on the same team—along with Hank Aaron and Darrell Evans—for the 1973 Braves. Two years later, no team wanted him on this continent, so he went to Japan and played for the Yomiuri Giants, ending the venerable Tokyo club's 10-year ban on foreign players. He returned to the majors as a part-time first baseman, playing for the Phillies in the 1977 NLCS. He tied a record with two pinch-hit grand slams for Philadelphia in 1978 and was rewarded by being traded to the Cubs. Johnson's last appearance in the major leagues came against Met Jerry Koosman, who'd gotten him to fly out to left field to end the 1969 World Series. This time, Kooz got Johnson to fly to right to end his career.

Johnson was prime managerial material. He'd been signed at 19 out of Texas A&M, earned a mathematics degree at Trinity College in Texas, and took computer classes at Johns Hopkins University at a time when the public's only knowledge of computers came from TV, mostly on *The Jetsons*. Johnson compiled data to make judgments, but he still managed a lot like his skipper in Baltimore, Earl Weaver. Johnson eschewed the bunt and played for the three-run homer, but computer data gave him a little better idea of who might hit one in a certain situation against a certain pitcher. Johnson also idolized Paul Richards, who'd helped build the "Kiddy Korps" in Baltimore. Twenty years later, the "Oriole Way" was on its way north.

Johnson first managed in the renegade Inter-American League in 1979, also taking over as GM and selling players to the major leagues and Japan at a profit. He profited more in real estate the next year, but Joe McIlvaine called and asked him to manage in the Mets system. It didn't take him long to see that the organization was busting out with talent.

Johnson managed at Class AA Jackson and Triple-A Tidewater in between a stint as a roving instructor. General manager Frank

Davey Johnson landed in the Mets dugout at about the same time that a handful of top prospects was getting ready to blossom. Photo courtesy of Getty Images.

Cashen, who, as Baltimore's GM, had traded away Johnson in 1972, considered his old second baseman the only man to run the club in New York in the mid-1980s. The team had nowhere to go but up.

"The New York Mets were in absolute shambles when I took over as manager in October 1983," Johnson said in his usual blunt style. "The team expected to lose....They had been losing for so many years that they took it for granted." Indeed, the Mets hadn't won more than 68 games since 1976. Johnson knew his best chance to win was with the young talent, but he gave the veterans on the pitching staff one last chance. They didn't make it.

Cashen let Johnson follow his plan, eating $1 million in salary in May with the release of pitchers Craig Swan and Dick Tidrow. Mike Torrez, the first Met to lose on Opening Day since 1974, was let go in June along with his $500,000 salary. New York called up Brent Gaff and Tom Gorman from Tidewater, moved Ed Lynch from the bullpen to the rotation, and traded three other youngsters to Cincinnati for hard-throwing Bruce Berenyi. Those four pitchers, all under 30, combined to go 27–16; none of the three released pitchers ever won another major league game. There was a reason the Mets had been named *Baseball America*'s Organization of the Year in 1983. It certainly wasn't because of the big-league club.

While the 1984 team also featured rookies Rafael Santana at shortstop and Mike Fitzgerald at catcher, plus the resurrection of the careers of infielders Wally Backman, Kelvin Chapman, and Ron Gardenhire, the three first-year players who really changed the fortunes of the Mets were pitchers Ron Darling, Sid Fernandez, and Dwight Gooden.

TRIVIA

Which Met broke Mike Vail's team-record 23-game hitting streak in 1984?

Answers to the trivia questions are on pages 187–189.

"My plan at the start of the season was for four of the five pitchers in my rotation to be young, with the expectations that three of the four would develop," Johnson recalled. "Then the next spring I would bring two more young kids up, and maybe one of them would make it, until I had five young, strong starters." It was a bold plan, and it actually worked quicker than expected. The team improved exponentially as a result.

TOP 10

Wins by a Mets Manager in a Season

	Manager	Year	Record	Finish
1.	Davey Johnson	1986	108–54	first place
2.	Davey Johnson	1988	100–60	first place
3.	Gil Hodges	1969	100–62	first place
4.	Davey Johnson	1985	98–64	second place
5.	Willie Randolph	2006	97–65	first place
6.	Bobby Valentine	1999	97–66	second place*
7.	Bobby Valentine	2000	94–68	second place*
8.	Davey Johnson	1987	92–70	second place
9.	Davey Johnson	1984	90–72	second place
10.	Bobby Valentine	1997	88–74†	third place
	Bobby Valentine	1998	88–74†	second place

*Indicates wild card winner.

Note: The 1990 club finished second in the NL East with a 91–71 record with two managers: Davey Johnson (20–22) and Bud Harrelson (71–49).

Darling and Walt Terrell, another member of Johnson's rotation, arrived in a trade for Lee Mazzilli in 1982. Darling won 12 games and Terrell 11 in 1984. Fernandez, acquired for two major leaguers from the Dodgers the previous December, joined New York in July and was impressive in 15 starts. It might have just been a nice story if not for Gooden; he made the Mets back-page news after years of being ignored.

The 19-year-old phenom captivated New York, winning 17 and setting the all-time rookie strikeout record. Johnson had come across Gooden while filling in as manager for a few games in 1982 in Kingsport, Tennessee. The raw Gooden, just 17, struck out a batter per inning in rookie ball. A year later at Class A Lynchburg, he went 19–4 and fanned 300 in 191 innings. He pitched for Johnson in Tidewater in two International League playoff games to help the Tides win a championship.

"After seeing him in those two games, I made up my mind that no matter where I managed the next year, Dwight would be my

TOP 10

Wins by a Mets Manager in a Career

Manager	Record	Percentage
1. Davey Johnson (1984–1990)	595–417	.588
2. Bobby Valentine (1996–2002)	536–467	.534
3. Gil Hodges (1968–1971)	339–309	.523
4. Yogi Berra (1972–1975)	292–296	.497
5. Joe Torre (1977–1981)	286–420	.405
6. Dallas Green (1993–1996)	229–283	.447
7. Willie Randolph (2005–2006)	180–144	.556
8. Casey Stengel (1962–1965)	175–404	.302
9. Bud Harrelson (1990–1991)	145–129	.529
10. Wes Westrum (1965–1967)	142–237	.375

Opening Day pitcher," Johnson said. He was wrong. Gooden pitched in the fourth game of the season for the Mets, but it took plenty of convincing for Cashen to let him be on the team at all in 1984.

Cashen was leery because of Tim Leary. Joe Torre had pushed hard and put the prized prospect on the team in 1981; he hurt his arm in his first start. The 1984 season was Leary's first extended major league action, and he went 3–3, mostly in relief. (He was traded to Milwaukee after the season.) Gooden had no physical problems. In fact, he was a physical marvel, pitching 218 innings and setting a rookie record with a major league best 276 strikeouts. By the All-Star Game, Gooden and Darling had 18 wins between them. Four Mets—Darryl Strawberry, Keith Hernandez, Jesse Orosco, and Gooden—were named All-Stars, the most in team history. Strawberry was the first Met to start the game since Dave Kingman in 1976. Gooden wowed the national audience by fanning the first three American League batters he faced. More impressive still was the fact that the Mets, second-to-last in the major leagues in runs scored after 81 games, had a half-game lead in the National League at the break.

The cobwebs were dusted off at Shea and "K" signs were every-where anytime Doc—the media had quickly picked up on the pitcher's childhood nickname—took the hill. The Mets reached 20 games over .500 on July 24, beating the Cardinals on a game-ending hit by Hernandez against Neil Allen, the man he'd been traded for a year earlier. The crowd roared and the stadium shook...on a Tuesday night. On Friday night, 51,000 watched a Gooden gem against the Cubs that pushed the lead to four and a half games. There were so many homemade signs of glee paraded around the field on "Banner Day" on Sunday that the club had to halt the parade to get the second game going. The series brought the most fans to Shea for a weekend in 12 years, but it also signaled a change in fortune. The Cubs swept the twin bill and took three of four to knock the Mets out of the .600 stratosphere.

The Cubs were enjoying their own resurgence under new manager Jim Frey, the hitting coach for the Mets the previous two years. Chicago's midseason acquisition, Rick Sutcliffe, was the only pitcher who could rival Gooden in 1984. Sutcliffe went 16–1 as a Cub, including three wins against the Mets. Second base sensation Ryne Sandberg also waylaid New York, knocking in nine runs against them for the year. Sutcliffe, Sandberg, and the Cubs took home the Cy Young, MVP, and NL East respectively; Gooden, Hernandez, and the Mets finished a respectable second in all three.

Johnson showed he was not afraid to try new things or move people around, whether on the roster or in the lineup. After Ray Knight was acquired August 28 for two future everyday players (Gerald Young and Manuel Lee), Johnson, fed up with a general lack of offense at shortstop, shifted Hubie Brooks to short and installed Knight at third. Johnson's talk with sullen George Foster resulted in an upswing in his production, as did flipping him in the lineup with Strawberry in August. Johnson lit into Strawberry for lackadaisical play during a six-game losing streak that put the Cubs in complete command. Strawberry had a huge September—nine homers and 30 RBIs—to help the team steady itself and finish with 90 wins, the second-highest total in club history.

A total of 1,842,695 fans crammed Shea—outdrawing the Yankees for the first time since Yankee Stadium reopened—the highest figure in Queens since 1973 and the "Ya Gotta Believe"

That Davey Johnson almost left the Mets for the Cardinals in 1983. He got into a dispute with Steve Schryver, new director of minor league operations, over his contract to manage Triple-A Tidewater. Johnson was contacted about taking over the Class AAA team of the Cardinals in Louisville and was offered more money. Lou Gorman, New York's vice president of baseball operations, intervened and made sure Johnson stayed. In the 1986 World Series, with Gorman serving as general manager of the Red Sox, he may have wished he'd let Johnson be.

pennant winner. The '84 Mets didn't win a pennant, but just making people believe in the Mets again was a miracle in its own right.

Although Johnson would put together an unprecedented string of successful seasons at Shea, including two division titles and a world championship, his first year was his most impressive work. Johnson finished second to Chicago's Frey in Manager of the Year balloting—Frey had ended a 39-year postseason drought for the Cubs—but Johnson was able to make that success last, a greater achievement than a trophy. A greater tribute is that of the 40 players on that 1984 team, four became major league managers, two became general managers, more than a dozen went into coaching at various levels, and four became announcers. Everyone learned more about the game by sitting in a Davey Johnson dugout. Or even by watching him from afar.

Unlucky at Cards

Nothing in the first 23 seasons of New York Mets baseball could have prepared fans for 1985. Not the string of 100-loss seasons, not the two miracle finishes that put the underdog club in the World Series, not the string of 90-loss seasons, and not even the fadeout to the Cubs in 1984. No, 1985 was like having the summer of your life and then finding out you needed an emergency operation. It would take all winter to recuperate. And you thought it was going to be the best year of your life.

It sure started that way. A year and a half after the Keith Hernandez deal, Frank Cashen brought in Gary Carter. It cost the Mets four homegrown players: local favorite Hubie Brooks, Mike Fitzgerald, who'd been New York's starting catcher in 1984, and top prospects Floyd Youmans and Herm Winningham. Brooks shifted to shortstop full time in Montreal and became the first player at the position to drive in 100 runs since Ernie Banks in 1960, but the deal improved the Mets' hitting, defense, and pitching staff all at once. Carter was the club's first power-hitting catcher, and he was a three-time Gold Glove winner and great game-caller as well. With Darryl Strawberry batting behind him, they combined to hit 61 home runs in 1985. The entire 1980 club hit just 61. Add in Howard Johnson, picked up out of Sparky Anderson's world championship doghouse in Detroit (for Walt Terrell), and the '85 club had the most potent lineup Shea Stadium had ever experienced.

The Mets already had a vocal leader in Keith Hernandez, who fed the press delicious quotes and could be found at his locker smoking and doing crossword puzzles. Carter was what many called the "rah-rah" type. He had plenty to cheer about.

With the addition of Gary Carter, the 1985 Mets had the franchise's most potent lineup ever.

Carter had three game-deciding hits in his first week with the club. Mets pitchers responded to their All-Star catcher, and New York started off 8–1. After a slow start, St. Louis battled the Mets for the division lead. It would stay like this until the final weekend of the season.

Outside forces stoked the drama. Strawberry tore ligaments in his thumb on May 11. Dwight Gooden looked human—briefly— losing consecutive starts and making his 24–4 season look all the more remarkable. Several Mets wore down in the relentless grind against the Cardinals. Carter caught 143 games despite needing knee surgery, reliever Jesse Orosco's arm tired under the workload, Doug Sisk couldn't find the plate, shortstop Ron Gardenhire was hurt constantly, trainer Steve Garland feared Wally Backman had a broken ankle at season's end, but the second baseman kept on playing.

As if playing shorthanded weren't enough, the Mets played some of the strangest games in club history in 1985. One was the worst loss since the club's founding—a 26–7 pasting in Philadelphia—and another featured one of the greatest products of the club's farm system, Nolan Ryan, now of the Astros, fanning Danny Heep to become the first pitcher to reach 4,000 strikeouts. Houston eventually won in 12 innings, one of eight games to go that long; the club played 22 extra-inning games in all. Two games went to the eighteenth.

On April 28 the Mets scored four times in the first inning at Shea and did not score again for 17 innings. Pittsburgh outhit the Mets, 18–6, despite Tom Gorman's seven shutout innings of relief. The strangest play of the afternoon, though, was a balk call in the ninth...on the first baseman. Hernandez started to charge in on a bunt and then dashed back to the bag to take a pickoff throw. Umpire Harry Wendelstedt told a furious Davey Johnson it was a rule. "He made it up," the manager fumed. Carter prevented a run from scoring on a brilliant play on a wild pitch that inning. Glacially slow, 41-year-old Rusty Staub, forced to play outfield for the first time in two years, made a sliding catch with two men on to save the game in the top of the eighteenth. The Pirates, who'd earlier used a pitcher to bat for an outfielder, brought both the infield and outfield in so close that Clint Hurdle's hard grounder in the bottom of the eighteenth went untouched and ended the game.

That was nothing compared with July 4. Two rain delays made it an early night for Dwight Gooden in Atlanta. The Mets still took a 7–4 lead, which they promptly blew in the eighth. Trailing in the

TRIVIA

When Dwight Gooden led both leagues in wins, ERA, and strikeouts in 1985, only six pitchers had ever achieved that before. What did the six pitchers have in common?

Answers to the trivia questions are on pages 187–189.

IF ONLY ... The Mets hadn't lost ten games against the Cardinals between April and September 1985. Three of those games were decided by one run, and two came in extra innings. One or two games might have made all the difference in the final week of the season.

ninth, Howard Johnson started the tying rally with a pinch-single off Bruce Sutter and came around to score the first of four runs he would score after his late-game entry at shortstop. HoJo's two-run homer gave the Mets a lead in the thirteenth, but it fell away on Terry Harper's game-tying two-run homer. By the eighteenth, Keith Hernandez, using a new stance on his father's recommendation, had hit for the cycle; Strawberry and Davey Johnson had been ejected for arguing; and the Mets had another lead. That's when the game really got strange. Pitcher Rick Camp, in the final year of a career in which he batted .074, stepped up with two outs and launched a home run. The Mets were so exhausted they were giddy. "The bench was rolling, Hernandez hid his face in his glove," Gorman said. "It was impossible." Hernandez said Gorman thought the batter was Gene Garber, who'd left the game an hour earlier.

Acting Mets manager Mel Stottlemyre wanted to take it to the next level and bring in left fielder Danny Heep to pitch, but Davey Johnson sent word to get starter Ron Darling ready. "We've come this far," Johnson said. "We ain't quitting now....We're not giving in on this one." The Mets scored five times against Camp, and the Braves were down to their last out yet again. But Darling allowed a pair of two-out walks and a single. Up stepped Camp with a chance to tie it once again with a long ball. This time, Camp struck out. It was 3:55 AM. Then the fireworks went off. It was Fireworks Night...and the Braves wanted to give the fans their money's worth.

The 1985 season was also bizarre because of what happened away from the field. A day after Darryl Strawberry hit three homers and was cheered madly at Wrigley Field on August 5, the players scattered because of a strike. A day after being called, the strike ended. (Though magnificently brief, future strikes wouldn't be so kind.)

An even bigger distraction was the Pittsburgh drug trials. Cocaine, the prevalent drug in baseball—and society—got so out of hand in Pittsburgh that players were purchasing the drug in the locker room at Three Rivers Stadium during games. Even the team's mascot, Pirate Parrot, was involved. Ten players, including former Mets John Milner and Lee Mazzilli, were called to testify before a grand jury about their drug use. Keith Hernandez, like the other players, was granted immunity from prosecution but not from public opinion. Hernandez, who'd long since quit using, said "40 percent" of players were involved with cocaine during the early 1980s. He later recanted this number. "How could I know what the percentage was?" he said months after the trial. "Whatever the number of users, I was one of them." (Hernandez would be punished with a six-figure fine.) Hernandez left the courtroom on September 6, flew to Los Angeles, entered the game in the tenth inning, and scored the winning run for the Mets three innings later.

The Mets returned home a half-game out of first place and then took two of three from the Cardinals for a one-game lead with 24 games left in the season. Over the next three weeks, the Cards benefited from white-hot Cesar Cedeño, who hit .434 with six home runs—including a game-winner against the Mets—after being acquired from Cincinnati on August 29. (The Mets had picked up released Larry Bowa August 20, but he hit .105 in the closing weeks of his career.) The Mets went 11–6 against the rest of the division until their rematch in St. Louis; the Cardinals were 15–3 and held first place by three games.

If the Mets lost once in the three-game set with the Cardinals, they were toast. Just three games remained on the schedule after the

By the NUMBERS
11—Games exceeding 18 innings in Mets history. While the Mets have gone 5–5 with one tie in those games, the three longest have been losses: to the Cardinals at Shea in 1974 in the NL's longest night game, to the Astros in a 24-inning shutout at the Astrodome in 1968, and to the Giants in a 23-inning game at Shea in 1964 (Gaylord Perry later claimed that he started using a spitter that day).

series. John Tudor, who had won 19 of his last 20 decisions, was moved up a day so he would face Ron Darling instead of Dwight Gooden, who'd wrapped up the Cy Young Award weeks earlier. Darling tossed nine shutout innings; Tudor lasted 10 innings. His replacement, Ken Dayley, fanned the first two Mets in the eleventh, but Strawberry ripped a momentous drive off the scoreboard clock at Busch Stadium for the only run of the game.

The next night, the Cardinals scored the first earned run off Gooden in 49 innings, but they did little else. The 5–2 win put the 20-year-old 20 games over .500. He led the league in wins, strikeouts, complete games, and innings. His 1.53 ERA was the lowest in the majors since 1968, the "Year of the Pitcher." If only Gooden could've pitched the next night, too.

While Davey Johnson had used his top two pitchers in the first two games, the exhausted and injured staff had just a couple of arms in shape for the most important game of the season. Johnson had no choice but to go with rookie Rick Aguilera—with rookie Roger McDowell following in the seventh—against Danny Cox. The Mets scored to open the game and loaded the bases with one out, but Cox pitched out of it. St. Louis tied it in the third when Terry Pendleton advanced two bases on a wild pitch—Carter couldn't find the ball—and scored on a force play. Rookie Vince Coleman, on his way to 110 steals before a tarp devoured him in the playoffs, singled in two runs to give the Cards the lead in the fourth. After the Mets pulled within a run, St. Louis extended the lead on a Willie McGee single. Coleman's speed kept Lenny Dykstra from scoring on a double in the seventh, but the Mets got a run in the eighth when HoJo began his career domination of Todd Worrell with a single. Ricky Horton relieved Worrell, and Davey Johnson countered by pinch-hitting for his pinch hitter. Ray Knight batted for Danny Heep and flied out, leaving no one to bat for Ron Gardenhire with two outs. Gardenhire struck out.

By the ninth inning, Mets fans tried to tell themselves this was just a walkthrough game from Septembers past; Joe Torre at the helm; the game meant nothing; Busch Stadium was packed because it was Appreciation Night in Hooterville (a Hernandez jibe at his old home). But it was no use. The game meant everything. And quickly there were two outs. Hernandez managed an infield hit, making him 5-for-5 on the night. Yet he never scored a run. Jeff Lahti came in and got Carter to fly to right. Next to Game 7 of the 1973 World Series, this was the toughest defeat in the first two dozen seasons of Metdom. Check that, this one was tougher. The '73 team came out of nowhere, stole a pennant, and almost beat the dynastic A's in the World Series; '85 ended in pain in Hooterville. The Cards officially clinched two days later and soon endured their own agonizing ending down the interstate in Kansas City. That didn't make anyone feel better in New York. Winter never seemed so long.

Mex: The Met You'd Want in Your Foxhole

By 1983 Keith Hernandez was a star. Not just a star, he was an All-Star, an All-Star with a brand-new World Series ring, a ring that he'd earned with eight RBIs against the Brewers in the 1982 World Series. And all he cost the Mets was Neil Allen.

Allen had often had physical issues during his first four seasons as a reliever with the Mets, but in 1983 his problems turned inward. His confidence shaken after a disastrous start to the season, Allen disappeared from the club for two days. His excuse—Allen said his wife had a medical emergency—turned out to be a lie. He confessed that he had an alcohol problem, but after the Mets admitted him to a treatment program, the medical staff felt that he was suffering from severe stress rather than alcoholism. So Allen became a starter for a team with the fewest wins in baseball.

Cardinals manager Whitey Herzog, working with ex-Mets GM Joe McDonald, was intrigued that Allen was suddenly available. He didn't have to look far to find the player he was angriest at just then: Keith Hernandez. Herzog was concerned that some Cardinals were involved in drugs. He asked the players to come forward and Herzog would see that they got help. Hernandez had often used cocaine, but he stopped on his own and didn't tell his manager. The Cards were stumbling, and Herzog was not a man who stood by and let things go sour. He acted. Impulsively.

It seemed like the perfect trade. Herzog dealt a player he thought had a cocaine problem who wouldn't admit it in return for a guy who said he had an alcohol problem and the doctors said he didn't. New York even threw in prospect Rick Ownbey. The trade was perfect...for the Mets.

Allen had some good moments for the Cardinals, like going 3–0 against the Mets the year of the trade, but it quickly became clear it was a steal. Herzog overlooked all the runs Hernandez saved with his superb glove, or the 1,217 hits he'd amassed in St. Louis, or how he'd keyed the Cardinals' comeback the previous fall in the sixth inning of Game 7 of the World Series, on his 29th birthday no less. Hernandez just had to decide if he wanted to stay in New York.

He had heard the trade rumors in St. Louis. The first was to the Astros for Verne Ruhle and future teammate Ray Knight. Hernandez let it be known he did not want to play in Houston because his mother's family lived near there. "Playing near family is tough. I would have simply played out my option with the Astros and left after one year." Not that he had great love for the Mets or Shea Stadium, what he called "the Siberia of baseball."

In the midst of a 94-loss season, the Mets had a Rookie of the Year in Darryl Strawberry, a poised 23-year-old September call-up named Ron Darling, speedster Mookie Wilson—who twice ended games in a four-day span in 1983 by scoring from second on ground-outs—and reports everywhere that the minor league system was about to churn out a bumper crop of ballplayers unseen in Queens since the late 1960s.

"I decided the Mets had a chance to be a better ballclub in 1984, maybe fourth place, but I also feared I would be signing up for six years of sixth place—dead last," Hernandez said. "It was a scary thought." After months of negotiations, Hernandez agreed to a contract worth $8 million, signing on for five years beyond the coming season. Those seasons would change his life and bring a crashing halt to the darkest period in franchise history.

Known as "Mex" because of his surname, even though his family came from Spain generations earlier and he didn't speak Spanish, Hernandez took charge in the clubhouse and on the field. The 1971 42nd-round draft pick turned 1979 NL co-MVP was the vital veteran presence on a Mets team full of talented prospects turned big leaguers. It worked. After splitting the first two games of the year, the '84 club went into the Astrodome and swept Houston there for the first time since 1966. New York never dipped below .500 after Opening Day. And by the time summer arrived, the Mets had taken over first place and the fans suddenly filling Shea thought the club might have its first league MVP. Yet Hernandez and the Mets finished second to Ryne Sandberg and the Cubs for both the NL East title and MVP. Hernandez hit .311, the highest by a Mets regular since Cleon Jones in 1971, and his .415 on-base percentage placed him third and his 97 walks second to Chicago's Gary Matthews.

The 1985 season was pressure-filled. The Mets were in a tooth-and-nail fight with Hernandez's old club that lasted all season, he was involved in a nasty divorce, and the Pittsburgh drug trials hung over his head. He had been very touchy about the subject of drugs since he arrived in New York, threatening a libel suit in 1984 after former executive director of the Major League Players Association Ken Moffett said Hernandez and St. Louis teammate Doug Bair had been involved with drugs while with the Cardinals. In Pittsburgh,

Keith Hernandez provided valuable veteran leadership for the young Mets in the mid-1980s, as well as a consistent bat and a Gold Glove.

By the NUMBERS

Most Gold Gloves since 1957, NL and AL

Pitcher: Jim Kaat, 16

Catcher: Ivan Rodriguez, 11

First Base: Keith Hernandez, 11

Second Base: Roberto Alomar, 10

Third Base: Brooks Robinson, 16

Shortstop: Ozzie Smith, 13

Outfield: Roberto Clemente, 12

Willie Mays, 12

Al Kaline, 10

Ken Griffey Jr., 10

Hernandez admitted in court that it was true. He had used cocaine on several occasions with at least five former Cardinals, but he stopped using the drug when he saw what it did to Lonnie Smith, who went into drug rehab about the same time Hernandez was traded to New York. The Mets were on the road during the trial—Hernandez missed two starts because of it—but the club returned from the West Coast just a half-game out of first place.

When the Mets faced the Cardinals on September 10, Hernandez faced the music. He stepped up to the plate in the first inning, awaiting the verdict from 50,000 fans at Shea. Hernandez received a long standing ovation. He stepped out of the box, took several deep breaths, and then he singled in Mookie Wilson. The Mets beat St. Louis and took over first place.

"They're great fans," Hernandez said about that first at-bat. "I just didn't expect that kind of ovation. It kind of got to me."

"As Keith goes, the team goes," manager Davey Johnson said of Hernandez as the trial approached. And using the short-lived official stat of game-winning RBI, the statement holds true. Hernandez was credited with 24 game-winners in 1985 and 129 for his career; both are the highest total during the time the stat was kept between 1980 and 1988.

By the NUMBERS

Mets Players Who Have Worn No. 17

Don Zimmer, 1962
Choo Choo Coleman, 1962–1963
Frank Lary,* 1964–1965
Dennis Ribant,* 1964
Jim Schaffer, 1965
Dick Stuart, 1966
Larry Elliot,* 1966
Don Bosch, 1967–1968
Rod Gaspar, 1969–1970
Teddy Martinez,* 1970–1973
Felix Millan,* 1974–1977
Gil Flores, 1978–1979
Jerry Morales, 1980
Ellis Valentine, 1981–1982
Keith Hernandez, 1983–1989
David Cone,* 1991–1992
Jeff McKnight,* 1993
Bret Saberhagen,* 1994–1995
Brent Mayne, 1996
Luis Lopez, 1997–1999
Mike Bordick, 2000
Kevin Appier, 2001
Satoru Komiyama, 2002
Graeme Lloyd, 2003
Jason Anderson, 2003
Wilson Delgado, 2004
Dae Sung Koo, 2005
Jose Lima, 2006

* Indicates the player also wore another number as a Met.

The Mets finished excruciatingly short of the Cardinals. In the 4–3 loss in St. Louis that left the Mets two games back with three to play, Hernandez went 5-for-5. After hitting .309 for the 98-win club, Hernandez told his manager, with even more bravado than usual, "If I can hit .300 with all the things I've been through this year, don't worry about me. I'll hit .300 until I die."

In February 1986 Major League Baseball suspended Hernandez and five others for one year. The gloom quickly lifted as Commissioner Peter Ueberroth offered to waive the suspensions if the players agreed to take drug tests for the remainder of their careers and contribute 10 percent of their salaries for the year—about $135,000 for Hernandez—to programs to combat drug abuse. Hernandez hit .310 and led the NL in walks in 1986. He placed fourth behind Philadelphia's Mike Schmidt in the MVP balloting (Gary Carter finished two votes ahead of Hernandez). Mex's real value came in the postseason.

Most of the Mets had never played in a postseason game. Carter got as far as the NLCS for Montreal in 1981, and Howard Johnson sat the bench for the '84 champion Tigers, but Hernandez was the only player on the team who'd started a World Series game. With reliever Jesse Orosco exhausted, and with the tying and winning runs on base in Houston in the sixteenth inning of Game 6 of the '86 NLCS, Hernandez didn't let his experience go to waste. As he often did, Hernandez went to the mound to talk to the pitcher. As the fans at the Astrodome roared, Hernandez told Orosco to stay with the breaking ball on Kevin Bass.

"Then I waited for Gary to get there," Hernandez recalled of the mound meeting with Orosco and Carter. "I was looking at Jesse, but I was talking to Kid. I want to loosen him up. So I just look at him and said, 'If you call one more fastball, we're gonna fight.'"

Orosco threw all sliders to Bass and finally struck him out to capture the pennant. Hernandez had gone just 1-for-7 in the game, but typically the hit was an RBI-double in the ninth and he scored the tying run, kicking across home plate with his fists clenched and shouting. This was certainly Keith Hernandez's team.

In Game 6 of the World Series, Hernandez was despondent in the clubhouse. The champagne had just been moved from the New

TRIVIA

Which starting pitcher got the Mets on the board with road wins in both the 1986 NLCS and World Series after the club began each series with losses?

Answers to the trivia questions are on pages 187–189.

York side to the Boston clubhouse (the Red Sox had forgotten their bubbly), and Hernandez sat smoking a cigarette, drinking a beer, and sure he'd just made the second-to-last out of the World Series. Then Carter singled. Rookie Kevin Mitchell, who'd been in the clubhouse with Hernandez and was getting ready to shower, threw on his pants, grabbed a bat as a pinch hitter, and singled. Ray Knight drove in Carter. And then came Mookie Wilson with the most famous at-bat in Mets history. Through it all, Hernandez stayed in the clubhouse, superstitiously feeling that if he moved, a Met would make an out and the Series would be over. He stayed. The Mets won.

The Mets were down three runs in Game 7 when Hernandez came up with the bases loaded in the sixth, the same inning and the same situation that he got the crucial hit against Milwaukee lefty Bob McClure in the deciding contest in 1982. Facing the southpaw Bruce Hurst four years later, Hernandez was 1-for-9 against him in the Series coming into the at-bat. His first two trips in Game 7, though, he'd lined out. This time he choked up another inch on the bat and lined a single to left-center to make it 3–2. An inning later, with the Mets now up two runs, Hernandez lifted a sacrifice fly to extend the lead to 6–3; that run would be all that kept the Mets in front after the Red Sox rallied in the eighth. With New York up by three runs once more in the ninth, Hernandez handled the putouts for the first two outs. Just as in Game 7 in St. Louis in '82, Hernandez became a spectator when a strikeout ended the Series. He celebrated so heartily that he just made the parade the next day.

The Mets never had a team captain in their first 25 seasons, and frankly had little reason to choose anyone. It's essentially a ceremonial rank; there are no special on-field/ice duties as in football or hockey. And the Mets never had anyone you'd feel the need to call captain. That Hernandez, the unquestioned team leader, spokesman, and notebook filler was also a Civil War buff made the rank and honor perfect. Carter was unhappy about it. The Mets named him co-captain in 1987 as both players' skills were starting to deteriorate, but everyone knew who the real captain was.

Hernandez did not hit .300 in any of his last three years with the Mets. He was a deserving All-Star in 1987, but he struck out 100 times for the only time in his career, and it marked the first time in a

DID YOU KNOW ... That in 1984 Keith Hernandez became the first Met to win the Silver Slugger Award? The award, started by Louisville Slugger manufacturer Hillerich & Bradsby, annually honors the best offensive player at each position in each league. Hernandez also won the inaugural National League award at first base for the Cardinals in 1980.

decade he fanned more times than he walked. The team pulled away to win the 1988 division title mostly without him. Hamstring injuries limited him to 95 games, his lowest number since his rookie year in 1975. He still led in the trenches, but was more like John Wayne leaning on a rifle after being wounded in *The Longest Day*. Hernandez did what he had to do, but when he injured his leg running in the muck in Game 3 of the ill-fated NLCS against the Dodgers, he never regained his stroke. He went 3-for-17 the rest of the series, and the Mets lost. "As Keith goes, the team goes."

The loss to a team they'd beaten 10 of 11 games during the season—and one that was among the league's weakest hitting clubs—lingered into 1989, as did injuries. Hernandez played only 75 games and hit .233, his lowest mark as a professional. Carter limped through the year as well. Both captains departed as free agents after the season. Hernandez was injured even more in Cleveland, playing for a club that was only slightly better than the Mets team he had joined in 1983. The Mets did not name another captain until John Franco in 2001.

Although Hernandez drifted from the game for several years, he remained popular, bringing his effusive character to an episode of *Seinfeld* that summed up his personality magnificently. "I'm Keith Hernandez," he cooed to himself as he went in to kiss his female foil, Elaine Benes (played by Julia Louis-Dreyfus). He remained one of the most popular Mets, and many wondered why, when they inducted him to the Mets Hall of Fame in 1997, the club didn't retire his number as well. That same day, light-hitting Luis Lopez homered for the only run of the game wearing Mex's number 17.

Hernandez joined the club's broadcast team in 1999, working a sporadic schedule but providing good theater because of his candor

Best Mets Trades

1. **Keith Hernandez** from the Cardinals, June 15, 1983: The Mets gave up Neil Allen, a good pitcher turned head case, and Rick Ownbey, a dubious pitching prospect. Whitey Herzog thought Hernandez was damaged goods, but he was wrong. Mex straightened himself out, bringing his skill and leadership to a franchise desperately needing both. Mets fans had to read the news repeatedly to believe it was true.

2. **Mike Piazza** from the Marlins, May 22, 1998: Rummage sale Florida did all right by this deal, getting Preston Wilson after sticking the Dodgers with a lot of dead weight along with Gary Sheffield to get Piazza for one week. But like Hernandez before him, Piazza brought star power to a team needing an hombre in the middle of the lineup. Piazza hit some of the most dramatic home runs in club history and became one of the most beloved Mets ever during seven-plus seasons in New York.

3. **Gary Carter** from the Expos, December 10, 1984: Very similar to the Piazza deal except the mid-1980s Mets were better than the late 1990s team. Both times the Mets needed a thumping catcher, and each time they got one. Hubie Brooks played 10 seasons and Mike Fitzgerald eight after the trade, but Carter's World Series ring as a Met put him over the top as a Hall of Famer.

4. **Ron Darling** and **Walt Terrell** from the Rangers, April 1, 1982: Lee Mazzilli was furious that he was traded for two minor leaguers. Sorry, Lee, this was Frank Cashen's first great deal. Darling was a top pitcher at Yale and a first-round pick able to learn quickly in the big leagues. He won 99 times as a Met and started three games in the 1986 World Series. Terrell, whom the Mets tried to draft to no avail in 1979, had two good years as a Met and was then traded for Howard Johnson. Mazzilli? He wound up on the '86 team, anyway.

5. **John Olerud** from the Blue Jays, December 20, 1996: For Robert Person. And the Blue Jays threw in $5 million. Thanks, eh? Olerud was nearly ruined when Cito Gaston tried to make him a home-run hitter in Toronto. The Mets left him alone, let him bat third, and he put together three of the most productive seasons in franchise history, plus the best defense at first since Keith Hernandez. Hearts broke when Olie signed with Seattle.

6. **David Cone** from the Royals, March 27, 1987: Because the "big name" in the five-player deal was backup catcher Ed Hearn, this is slightly more of a steal than the Sid Fernandez heist of '83. Cone was a workhorse, winning 80 games in just over five seasons as a Met with a 3.08 ERA in his first stint with the team before going 1–3 in five games in a brief 2003 return. Conie twice led the league in strikeouts and missed a third K crown by only one after the Mets traded him out of the NL.

7. **Sid Fernandez** from the Dodgers, December 8, 1983: El Sid came to the Mets for reliever Carlos Diaz and utility man Bob Bailor. L.A. tried to throw cold water on the deal by saying Fernandez had a sore arm. Fat chance. As a Met, Fernandez won 98 games, had a 3.15 ERA, and opponents hit just .204 against him. His bullpen work in Game 7 of the 1986 World Series, though, may have been his finest moment with the club.

8. **Donn Clendenon** from the Expos, June 15, 1969: New York gave up four prospects, including Steve Renko, to get Clendenon from Montreal at the deadline, but that 1969 lineup would have been bone dry of miracles without Clendenon in the middle of it. He provided protection for Cleon Jones and a veteran presence on a team full of kids.

9. **Al Leiter** from the Marlins, February 6, 1998: One of three prospects-for-professionals trades between the Mets and Marlins over a six-month span. (Florida got A.J. Burnett in this deal.) Leiter grew up loving the Mets and gave them everything he had at the top of the rotation. Too bad he didn't retire sooner as he once said he would because it ended ugly at Shea, otherwise he'd be in the SNY booth.

10. **Tommie Agee** and **Al Weis** from the White Sox, December 15, 1967: Give an assist to new manager Gil Hodges, acquired via trade from the Senators just two months earlier, for pushing for this deal by Bing Devine. Hodges knew these two players from the American League. Agee was a slugging center fielder with a superb glove, prone to slumps but he excelled in big moments. And the Mets couldn't have won without Weis platooning at second in '69.

Note: It's too early to tell on several Omar Minaya trades just yet.

about his exploits on and off the field and his ability to honestly critique the team in front of him. Of course, candor has its drawbacks. The man whose long-running hostility with Darryl Strawberry led to a memorable fight while taking the team photo in 1989 had to apologize for writing that the 2002 team quit on Bobby Valentine (even though it was obviously true). His comments about Padres masseuse Kelly Calabrese being in the dugout in San Diego in 2006 also caused problems. That is the way Hernandez has always been. His 1986 book, *If at First*, took shots at everyone associated with the team or his career. How did that play in the clubhouse? The team won its first world championship in 17 years. Even today, when fans look for a mouthpiece about the glory years a generation past, or for analysis, or a good joke, they look to Keith Hernandez...just as they did when the Mets went from NL East doormat to divisional power.

One Oh Eight, Eighty-Six

Unlike agonizing 1985, with its drama and heart-rending finish, 1986 cuddled a Mets fan and whispered, "Nothing bad's gonna happen. Nothing bad." A Mets fan couldn't believe this type of optimism. All good things either came crashing down or were won after countless hours of angst. Even the first two pennant-winning Mets clubs endured many moments of doubt. This team would be different. Oh, really? Really.

- Keith Hernandez was suspended for one year for his part in baseball's cocaine culture of the early 1980s in St. Louis. Instead of sitting out the year, he was giving the option of paying a fine—a hefty one—and he batted .310 in 149 games.
- The 1986 Mets set nearly every team batting mark to that time: average (.263), runs (783), hits (1,462), doubles (261), home runs (148), and RBIs (730). They led the league in runs, hits, batting, walks (631), on-base percentage (.339), and slugging percentage (.401).
- The 1986 Mets might not have set team marks on the mound—the franchise already had a good reputation in that regard—but they led the major leagues in fewest home runs allowed (103) and lowest ERA (3.11).
- Dwight Gooden wasn't anywhere close to as overpowering as the 1985 Doc, but he still went 17–6 with a 2.84 ERA and 200 strikeouts.
- The Mets had six pitchers win in double figures. Bob Ojeda, Ron Darling, Sid Fernandez, and Gooden each won at least 15; reliever Roger McDowell won 14. They were durable, too.

By the NUMBERS **21½**—The number of games the Mets finished ahead of the Phillies in 1986. It was the largest margin in the National League since the Pirates won by 27½ games in 1902, the year before the first World Series between the NL and AL.

The aforementioned starting quartet each went over 200 innings and McDowell became the first Met to appear in 75 games. Rick Aguilera, a 1983 draft choice, went 10–7 for the second straight year.

This team was built to dominate. The 1985 team won 98 games, so no overhaul was needed. The new pieces were designed to fill specific needs. Southpaw Ojeda came over from the Red Sox in a trade involving eight players, most notably Calvin Schiraldi. Ojeda prospered with the change of scenery and getting away from Fenway Park's short fence in left field. He was one of four Mets pitchers to start the season with a 5–0 record. Tim Teufel also came over from the American League. The former Twin gave the Mets something they'd never had in a second baseman: power. He also produced from the right side, something switch-hitting Wally Backman never could. That second base platoon begat limited job sharing by Howard Johnson and Rafael Santana taking turns at shortstop, George Foster and Danny Heep in left, and Lenny Dykstra and Mookie Wilson in center. The flexibility in the lineup made the Mets far more formidable offensively.

Davey Johnson, armed with a three-year extension, wasn't concerned about hurt feelings. These were grown men. And he had no intention of finishing second for the third straight year.

The season began in Pittsburgh. New York would pummel the Pirates 17 of 18 times as initiation to rookie manager Jim Leyland. (The only Bucs blemish in 1986 came in the first game of a makeup doubleheader in June, when leadoff man Barry Bonds hit his second career home run.) The Mets reached their nadir at the home opener when they fell to the Cardinals in 13 innings. The Mets were 2–3 with Randy Niemann, the only pitcher who would spend all season with the club and finish with a losing record, absorbing two defeats in the first five games.

The Mets embarked on an 11-game winning streak, tying a franchise record and laying waste to the National League East by the end of April. New York swept through St. Louis in style. The Mets tied the series opener in the top of the ninth on a home run by Howard Johnson off Todd Worrell; they won an inning later. On Saturday, a ninth-inning Cardinals rally was scotched on Wally Backman's diving stop that turned a game-winning hit into a game-ending double play...on national television.

"I could see the frustration in their faces," Keith Hernandez said of the Cardinals after the four-game sweep. "You can see the way they look as they make a right and head back toward their dugout."

Lefty Bob Ojeda was more than happy to get away from Fenway Park, and he provided a key piece to the puzzle that was to bring home the 1986 championship.

By the NUMBERS

5—Number of Mets on the All-Star team, the most in franchise history. Four were starters: Dwight Gooden, Gary Carter, Keith Hernandez, and Darryl Strawberry. Sid Fernandez struck out the side in his inning of work.

Yes, the '86 Mets were cocky. They were involved in brawls, blowouts, and barroom brouhahas. They had the ex-boxer Knight taking on massive Dodgers reliever Tom Niedenfuer in May. David Palmer, a former teammate of Gary Carter's, resented "the Kid's" fist-pumping curtain call after his first of two home runs in the first two innings, so he drilled Darryl Strawberry with the next pitch. When Straw came calling, Palmer threw his glove at the outfielder's face. Nothing Palmer threw that night was effective. Just after the All-Star Game, a celebration of the birth of Teufel's first child turned into a fracas with off-duty Houston police officers; four Mets were arrested. New York lost the next three games at the Astrodome, including a 15-inning affair that was the longest game the team played all season...but they'd take it later at the dome in October.

Even after a bad series in Houston, the Mets were still 60–28 midway through July. They swept the next series in Cincinnati, punctuated by Knight grappling with sinewy Reds speedster Eric Davis after a hard slide. Ejections forced the Mets to put pitchers in the outfield as the game dragged on, but—surprise!—they won anyway.

The Mets had barrel-chested rookie Kevin Mitchell starting games at shortstop in Davey Johnson's "power lineup." Mitchell played five other positions, too. He spent most of his time in left field, as did Mookie Wilson. Incumbent George Foster suggested his benching was racially motivated, although it was pointed out that Mitchell, Wilson, and Foster were the same color. Foster was cut on August 7. Davey Johnson had been calling for the move even before the Foster flap, but the incident caused a few singed feelings in the club about the way it was handled. Lee Mazzilli, one-time Shea heartthrob and now just holding on as a pinch hitter, took Foster's place on the roster.

Lenny Dykstra, playing 138 games in center field, took over the leadoff spot against right-handers and batted .295 in his first full season in the majors. Though not known for his arm, he started one of the most unlikely double plays of the year to end the most successful West Coast trip (8–1) in club history. After blowing a 5–0 lead earlier in the game, the Mets' one-run lead in the bottom of the eleventh in San Diego looked shaky. Tim Flannery singled to center as Garry Templeton raced to the plate from second base. Playing shallow, Dykstra fired to catcher John Gibbons, who absorbed a collision and held on to the ball. Hearing pitcher Doug Sisk call for him to throw to third base, Gibbons got off the ground and threw to Howard Johnson to nail Flannery to end the game.

Set to clinch after just 139 games, the club experienced its worst slump of the year: six losses in seven games. After getting swept in Philadelphia, a two-game split in St. Louis denied the Mets the pleasure of clinching in the place where it had all ended in anguish a year before. On the bright side, it allowed them to celebrate at home. Dwight Gooden, whose emergence in 1984 had signaled a sea change in the club's fortunes, captured the clincher with his 56th career win at the tender age of 21. The fans tore the place apart. The team celebrated with gusto, too.

TRIVIA

Which future Met made the last out of the division-clinching game at Shea Stadium on September 17, 1986?

Answers to the trivia questions are on pages 187–189.

A week later, the Mets won their 100th game. They beat Ed Lynch, the Brooklyn native who'd been a Met for five years only to be traded to the Cubs. (Lynch had also endured the celebration at Shea from the opposing side.) The Mets reeled off eight wins in their last nine games to finish with a 108 wins, eight more than the 1969 club.

The Mets won in very conceivable fashion. They shut out opponents 11 times, they beat them in one-run games 29 times (against 20 losses), and, not surprisingly, won more extra-inning games (13) than any Mets team in history. They'd need all that extra-inning practice for October.

"And a Ground Ball Trickling..."

After 13 years of waiting, many of them as the dregs of the National League, the Mets finally returned to the postseason in 1986. Heavily hyped and supremely confident, the Mets would have one of the most torturous and thrilling October marches since the start of the two-tiered postseason format in 1969, a year that still brought a smile to the face of every Mets fan. The 1986 juggernaut seemed like an easy choice to win it all on paper. That paper would be scuffed, nailed, rained on, frozen, stomped, cursed, rained on some more, and, finally, doused with beer and champagne. They had 'em all along.

The 108-win Mets went to Houston to play a franchise also born in 1962. Mike Scott had shown no signs of ever being an ace during his four-year, 14–27 Mets apprenticeship that ended with a 1982 trade for Danny Heep. Now he was "Great Scott," the best pitcher in the league. Scott struck out 306 batters, averaging 10 strikeouts and 5.95 hits per game, and, to cap it, he threw a no-hitter to clinch Houston's second-ever postseason berth (the Mets had clinched number three eight days earlier). All this came after Scott learned the split-fingered fastball from Roger Craig, who'd set a dubious mark for consecutive losses while an original Met.

Scott and the Astros overlooked the miles of Mets media clippings and controlled Game 1. Dwight Gooden, with an 8–1 career mark against Houston going in, gave up a home run to Glenn Davis leading off the second inning. That was the ballgame. Scott threw 126 pitches, had two strikes on 24 of 33 batters he faced, and fanned 14 in the 1–0 win. Bobby Ojeda tossed his own gem for the Mets the next night to even the series. Bobby O.'s complete-game effort, despite allowing 10 hits, would be much appreciated in the days to come.

Game 3, the first postseason game at Shea since the 1973 World Series, featured two Mets comebacks. Darryl Strawberry roped a three-run homer to tie the game after the Astros grabbed a big early lead. Then, in the ninth inning, Wally Backman laid down a bunt and was ruled safe despite nearly running to the Whitestone Bridge to avoid the tag. Lenny Dykstra, who'd entered the game in the seventh, lined a Dave Smith forkball into the bullpen in right field. Shea Stadium erupted like a volcano that had been dormant for 13 years.

Scott quieted the place down the next night, holding New York to just three hits and tying the series. The Mets were convinced he was cheating and seemed to focus more on collecting scuffed baseballs than on trying to hit them. "If [Scott] doesn't scuff it up," wrote Ron Darling, pitcher turned columnist in the *New York Daily News*, "he's got some of the greatest stuff I've seen in a long time." Gary Carter, who'd caught Scott's scuffed pitches in the All-Star Game, was most adamant about the pitcher's guilt and the least able to hit him: 0-for-8 with five strikeouts and one ball out of the infield against Scott. (Twenty years later, Carter told a New York radio station that Scott had admitted his chicanery when the two retired players met at a golf tournament.) The Mets pushed across a run to end Scott's NLCS record for

TRIVIA

Who was first Met to serve as a designated hitter?

Answers to the trivia questions are on pages 187–189.

most consecutive scoreless innings at 16⅔, but it was small consolation. The Mets were convinced that if there was a Game 7, they had no chance against Scott. They had to win the next two.

Nolan Ryan, in his first postseason game at Shea since his save for the Mets in the 1969 World Series, was brilliant in Game 5. Darryl Strawberry's line drive to the corner just cleared the 338-foot sign in right field in the fifth inning. It was New York's first hit, and one of just two in nine innings against Ryan, who fanned 12 and walked one. Gooden went 10 innings and, though not nearly as masterful as Ryan, kept the game tied. Gary Carter, 1-for-21 in the series as he stepped up to the plate in the twelfth inning, singled in Wally Backman with the winning run to give the Mets the lead in the series.

DID YOU KNOW . . . That because of a rainout in New York on Monday, October 13, Games 5 and 6 of the 1986 NLCS were played on consecutive days, covering 28 innings, in cities 1,200 miles apart? The games, both begun during the day, totaled 8 hours and 27 minutes of baseball. Jesse Orosco won both a little more than 24 hours apart.

The next day's game would be the subject of an entire book, and a game that still may be the most thrilling contest in Mets history. It was an amalgam of the first five games; the only thing missing was Mike Scott. And his presence lingered over the proceedings in the Astrodome, incentive for the Mets to do everything possible to keep him from taking the mound in Game 7.

A seventh game looked like a foregone conclusion after the first inning. Houston scored three quick runs off Ojeda, and it could have been more if Alan Ashby hadn't missed a suicide squeeze. Bob Knepper, meanwhile, sailed through the Mets lineup. He averaged just 11 pitches per inning, allowed two hits, and walked one in eight innings. The second half of the game kicked off in the ninth.

Dykstra, batting for Rick Aguilera, lashed a triple to center. He trotted home on a hit by Mookie Wilson, who then scored on a Keith Hernandez double. Dave Smith came on in relief and blew a Knepper victory for the second time in the series. Smith walked two batters, stomping around the mound at several borderline calls. Ray Knight, shouting expletives at the argumentative Astros, lifted a sacrifice fly to tie the game.

Roger McDowell pitched five innings in relief, allowing just one hit. When the Mets scored in the fourteenth on Backman's single, Jesse Orosco entered. The worn-out lefty allowed a game-tying home run off the foul-pole screen to Billy Hatcher, but he fought on. Orosco threw 54 pitches, with fans in Houston and New York living and dying on each one. After the Mets took the lead with three in the sixteenth, Orosco gave two runs back. Keith Hernandez walked over and not so calmly threatened bodily harm if a fastball was thrown to Kevin Bass. Bass missed a slider, and the Mets had the pennant.

The Boston Red Sox held the other pennant. They had taken it from the California Angels forcibly, rallying with two outs in Game 5 on a Dave Henderson home run when the Angels—and manager Gene Mauch—were seemingly assured of a World Series appearance at long last. The Red Sox took the last three games, but the effort had been as exhausting as anything the Mets had done. First baseman Bill Buckner, a .282 lifetime hitter in 156 games against the Mets as a National Leaguer, had strained his right Achilles tendon in Boston's clinching game. Agate type in the paper read, "His status for the World Series is questionable."

The Red Sox perked up for Game 1. They played in arctic conditions at Shea Stadium, and the only run of the game was scored on an error by Tim Teufel. A ballyhooed pitching match-up the next night

The Mets' march through the 1986 postseason was one of the most memorable—and agonizing—in playoff history. Here they celebrate their Game 6 victory in that season's World Series. Photo courtesy of Getty Images.

featured 21-year-old Gooden against Roger Clemens, 24. In their young careers, both pitchers had already had seasons of 24–4 and leading the league in ERA, Gooden in 1985 and Clemens in '86. Both were very hittable in Game 2. Gooden went just five innings, and Clemens didn't even last that long, yanked two outs shy of qualifying for a World Series win with a 6–2 lead. Steve Crawford, without a win during the regular season, relieved and was credited with the victory as Boston romped, 9–3. As the game dragged on, the crowd at Shea dwindled to its pre-renaissance size. Hawkers in the parking lot eagerly slashed prices to get rid of items they weren't sure they'd have another chance to sell. The idea of a Game 6 seemed very remote.

Davey Johnson gave the Mets the next day off in Boston. They'd been to Fenway Park for a charity exhibition six weeks earlier; they'd seen the big wall. The exhausted Mets were grateful they didn't have to go to the Fenway media circus. "To me that was the turning point," Carter said. Boston's Game 3 starter, Oil Can Boyd, never at a loss for words, told the media, "Being down 2–0 and not checking out our ballpark, that doesn't show us too much respect." Boyd's boasts about "mastering those guys," made the Mets do a slow burn as they watched from the Sheraton.

Lenny Dykstra started Game 3 with a thunderbolt. His home run off Boyd begat a four-run rally as the Red Sox even botched a rundown play. Ojeda, despised by his old teammates in Boston, made the lead stick. "That game was the proudest I've ever been on the baseball field," Ojeda later said.

The Mets hammered Al Nipper the next night to even the World Series. Carter launched two home runs, and Ron Darling tantalized Boston all night as the Red Sox left 11 men on base. Bruce Hurst confounded the Mets in Game 5 to gain his second win of the Series. Also for the second time, Gooden was awful. The Red Sox were one win away from the title, but at least there would be a Game 6.

By the NUMBERS

6—The most years of major league experience among Mets pitchers on the October roster, shared by Bob Ojeda and Jesse Orosco. None of the nine Mets pitchers on the roster had ever appeared in a postseason game before 1986.

DID YOU KNOW... That the 1986 Mets hit .189 against the Astros in the NLCS, making them the first team in history to win a league pennant after hitting below .200 in a playoff series? In three of their victories, they did not hold a lead until the ninth inning or later. Houston hit .218.

On October 25, 1986, Shea Stadium shook so much that clouds of dust and sediment fell from the rafters. But one of the loudest moments came in the top of the first with one on, one out, and Bob Ojeda on the mound. Michael Sergio, an actor on the soap opera *Loving*, appeared from the sky, landing in his parachute in fair territory behind the pitcher's mound, about where a good drag bunt might stop rolling. Sergio and his "Go Mets" banner were quickly removed. He would eventually spend three weeks at a correctional facility, prompting a Banner Day outcry of "Free Sergio" in 1987. His arrival at Shea in '86, though, was a clear indication to the 55,078 in the park and 26 million watching at home that this wasn't going to be just any game. As if they needed Michael Sergio to tell them.

The Mets fell behind a few minutes later, but caught two breaks because of Jim Rice. The 33-year-old slugger somehow did not score from first on a two-out double in the first, and he was thrown out at the plate by the weak-armed Mookie Wilson to end the seventh. Still, the Red Sox had a 3–2 lead, aided by Ray Knight's error. The Mets were in trouble. They'd already pinch-hit for shortstop Rafael Santana and replaced him with 22-year-old Kevin Elster, who'd been at Class AA Jackson in August. Elster made the last out of the seventh, but it turned out to be the last pitch Roger Clemens threw. Despite 135 pitches, a popped blister, and a torn fingernail that affected his grip, he still wanted to pitch. Boston manager John McNamara sent up a pinch hitter in a moment of infamy in the overstuffed book of Red Sox misfortune.

Former Met Calvin Schiraldi replaced Clemens and immediately allowed a single to Lee Mazzilli as a pinch hitter. Schiraldi then tried for a force play on Dykstra's bunt, but all hands were safe on a bad throw. A sacrifice and an intentional walk brought up Gary Carter. Schiraldi fell behind 3–0, and Carter, who would drive in nine runs in the Series, had the green light. He lined to left to bring in the tying run.

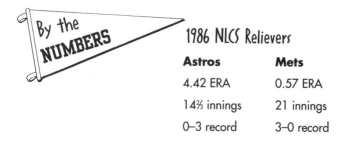

By the NUMBERS

1986 NLCS Relievers

Astros	Mets
4.42 ERA	0.57 ERA
14⅔ innings	21 innings
0–3 record	3–0 record

Elster made an error in the top of the ninth, but nothing came of it. The Red Sox screwed up a bunt in the bottom of the ninth, and the Mets followed by messing up their own sacrifice situation. (Howard Johnson—batting for Elster—couldn't lay down a bunt and then whiffed.) Two pitches into the tenth inning, Dave Henderson homered to left field off Rick Aguilera. After consecutive strikeouts, Wade Boggs doubled, and Marty Barrett drove in the insurance run. Bill Buckner was hit by a pitch—a perfect opportunity for John McNamara to replace him with the faster and better-fielding Dave Stapleton—but Billy Buck stayed on first base. After Rice made the third out, it was, as David Letterman liked to say, "Wake the kids and phone the neighbors" time in New England. For Mets fans, what they'd seen so far had them thinking that this was going to make the bitter finish in 1985 seem like a picnic.

Schiraldi quickly retired Backman and Hernandez in the bottom of the tenth inning. Then something happened that not even Bobby Thomson, or dem Bums, or the Yankees mystique, or even the Miracle Mets had ever managed. Of the first 81 World Series, the only team facing elimination in Game 6 or later that had gone from season-ending defeat to victory in their last at-bat had been the Red Sox. Boston had rallied in the tenth inning off New York Giants legend Christy Mathewson to win the 1912 World Series in brand-new Fenway Park. The Royals had done it to St. Louis in the 82nd World Series, in 1985. Neither of those situations, however, began with two outs and no one on—or with a congratulations sign for the visiting team on the Diamond Vision scoreboard.

The sign quickly came down. So did the Reds Sox. Carter singled to left. Pinch hitter Kevin Mitchell followed with a single to center. Knight blooped an 0–2 pitch to center to score Carter and send

Mitchell to third. Bob Stanley replaced Schiraldi. Mookie Wilson stepped to the plate, and the sound of "Moooook!" rose on top of the perpetual roar. A notorious free swinger, Mookie had a 2–2 count when Stanley went for the kill. His palmball darted out of control. Mookie jackknifed, and the ball went under him and found its way to the backstop. Mitchell scored, the game was tied, and the noise was deafening. Mookie kept fouling them off—six in all—before he finally put a ball in play.

No one painted the "word picture" better than the voice of the Mets' Bob Murphy, on radio station WHN: "Mookie Wilson still hopes to win it for New York...3–2 the count...And the pitch by Stanley...And a ground ball trickling...It's a fair ball. It gets by Buckner! Rounding third is Knight...The Mets will win the ballgame...They win! They win!"

They had to win one more game and had to wait one more day because of a rainout. The extra day enabled Bruce Hurst to pitch for Boston, keeping Oil Can Boyd on the bench. The Red Sox rocked Darling and took a 3–0 lead. The story the nation wanted to hear, how the Red Sox finally won, would now be even sweeter coming after a legendary Game 6 collapse. And it would come at the expense of that arrogant *other* team from New York.

Keith Hernandez, the face of that other team, singled in two runs off Hurst. Carter brought in the tying run. Series MVP Ray Knight broke the tie in the seventh. Darryl Strawberry helped put it away with a homer in the eighth. Orosco fanned Marty Barrett, and his glove went into orbit. Fans in other towns remember the '86 Series for the Buckner gaffe; Mets fans remember what came after. Orosco on his knees on the front page of the *Daily News*, one word saying all that could be said: "YES!"

Messy Jesse

Twins owner Calvin Griffith was adept at trading pricey veterans for low-cost prospects, but that rare deal that went the other way proved a little trickier. Minnesota had the Mets over a barrel. Jerry Koosman wanted to go back to his home state, and, after suffering through horrific seasons and no support in 1977 and 1978, the Mets had every reason to believe the soon to be 37-year-old Koosman was serious with his threat to retire if the deal didn't happen. Mets general manager Joe McDonald already had pitcher Greg Field coming back in the trade and was working on the player to be named later.

McDonald knew of a first-year left-hander who'd had a 1.13 ERA for the Twins at Elizabethtown in the Appalachian League. The second-round pick in 1978 out of Santa Barbara Junior College had good breaking stuff and seemed durable enough. This was news to Calvin Griffith. His adopted father, Clark Griffith, had shrewdly run the Washington Senators for half a century. The Old Fox had even traded his son-in-law, player/manager and future Hall of Famer Joe Cronin, for enough money to keep the franchise solvent in the Depression. Calvin Griffith wasn't that dynamic. When the young pitcher's name came up, Griffith used his poker face: "Who's Orosco?" The Mets dealt the last remaining star of their glory days, getting back a key part of their future. And Griffith could get back to the hard work of figuring out how to trade Rod Carew...for prospects.

Jesse Orosco spent eight seasons as a Met, winning the same number that he lost, which was also the same number he wore on his back (47). He appeared 372 times for the team and earned a then-club

Jesse Orosco provided the Mets with their best closer since Tug McGraw.

record 107 saves, not counting his glorious run in October 1986. The postseason, though, was the furthest thing from Orosco's mind when he arrived at his first spring training in 1979.

The 21-year-old Californian was a non-roster invitee with 20 games of experience in rookie ball. The Mets weren't picky. Many arms would be needed to get through a season of pounding by the likes of the Pirates, Phillies, Expos—you get the idea. After making the team based on six spring training appearances, Orosco debuted by inducing Bill Buckner to fly out to conclude the team's Opening Day victory. By June, his good outings had yielded to bad, and he was back in the minors. He didn't return until the end of the 1981 season. When Orosco came back, he was tentative, especially against the big guns. George Bamberger, a pitcher's manager whose pitchers never managed very well, built Orosco's confidence by giving him the ball consistently. He appeared 54 times in 1982, more than any Met. He learned how to shake off 10 losses, and his 2.72 ERA was the best of any Met who appeared in 10 or more games. What really helped, though, was getting rid of Neil Allen.

Allen, nine months younger than Orosco, had also made the Mets out of spring training in 1979, but when the team wanted to send him to the minors, Allen got hurt. With nowhere else to turn, Joe Torre tried him in the bullpen when he came back. Allen racked up 23 wins and 67 saves over four seasons for a team without many leads to protect. A colon infection in June 1982 made Allen too weak to be of much use, and the next year a series of problems led Bamberger to make him a starting pitcher. Allen was dealt to the Cardinals with Rick Ownbey for Keith Hernandez. It wasn't just the greatest deal in franchise history, the bullpen door now swung wide for Orosco. He ran through it with incredible frequency and remarkable efficiency.

Bamberger quit and Frank Howard took over, but the big man wasn't afraid to use the now 26-year-old lefty. Orosco made the All-Star team, the first Mets reliever tabbed since Tug McGraw in 1972. And Orosco was just warming up. (Actually, he both warmed up and came in to get an out during the All-Star Game, striking out Ben Oglivie.) From July 22 to August 24, Orosco put together 27⅔ consecutive scoreless innings over 15 appearances. He was Player of the Week twice in a row. He won two games in one day against Pittsburgh, tossing five innings in the July 31 twin bill. Orosco appeared in 62 games, saved 17, won a team-best 13 times, logged a career-high 110 innings, and had a miniscule 1.47 ERA. He finished third in the Cy Young voting and even garnered a few Most Valuable Player votes. Not bad for a guy on a last-place team.

Under new manager Davey Johnson, Orosco pitched 23 fewer innings but was run out there just as often in 1984. Orosco became the first Met to surpass 30 saves and he was named an All-Star again. What's more, on July 27 he saved a 2–1 win over the Cubs by rookie phenom Dwight Gooden to put the Mets 22 games over .500 and four and a half games in front in the National League East. (A year earlier on that date, the Mets were 25 games under .500 and 14½ games out.) August and September weren't as kind to the overachieving '84 Mets, who wound up second with 90 wins. It also marked the first full season in Orosco's major league career in which his club didn't *lose* 90 games and finish in last place.

The Mets were loaded for bear in 1985, but Orosco's aim was a little off. Although he appeared in 54 games, a tender elbow made every outing a crapshoot. Johnson, who relied heavily on Orosco in tight situations, admitted, "I have to be careful how I use him." His adventures on the mound earned him the title "Messy Jesse." His 2.73 ERA, the highest since his rookie season, was still relatively clean. Orosco and Roger McDowell tied for the team lead with 17 saves as New York finished three agonizing games behind St. Louis.

The 1986 club cruised to a double-digit lead by the start of July and racked up 108 wins. Orosco blew eight saves, the same number as 1985, but that didn't even cause a ripple. On July 22 the Mets and Reds staged a surreal contest, with Orosco spending more time in the outfield than on the mound. A fight in the tenth inning led to the third ejection of the game. The Mets were caught short—the major

By the NUMBERS

Jesse Orosco's Major League–Record 1,252 Games, by Team

Games Pitched	Team	Years
372	Mets	1979, 1981–1987
146	Dodgers	1988, 2001–2002
171	Indians	1989–1991
156	Brewers	1992–1994
336	Orioles	1995–1999
6	Cardinals	2000
42	Padres	2003
15	Yankees	2003
8	Twins	2003

DID YOU KNOW . . . That the Mets were swept in four doubleheaders in five days in September 1979? The team scored a total of 11 runs while losing to the Cubs (twice), Expos (four games), and Cardinals (twice). They completed an 0–9 home stand at Shea with a 10-inning loss to St. Louis on September 23.

leagues had a 24-man roster at the time—so Orosco moved from the mound to right field and McDowell came in to pitch. The two alternated places for the next four innings, with Mookie Wilson also moving around in the outfield based on who was up for Cincinnati. Orosco caught a fly ball, worked out a walk, and scored a run in the fourteenth as the Mets won.

Orosco broke Tug McGraw's club record with his 86th career save on August 9 as New York rallied from a 6–1 deficit in Montreal. He pitched 81 innings in 58 appearances.

Orosco picked up the win in Game 3 of the NLCS on Lenny Dykstra's two-run, game-ending home run in the bottom of the ninth. When he appeared in Game 5, the series was even. With former Met Mike Scott dominating New York in both Houston wins, the Mets desperately wanted to win Games 5 and 6 and avoid unhittable Scott in a deciding contest. Orosco helped the Mets reach the first part of the goal with two perfect frames in a 12-inning win. That left the small matter of Game 6 in Houston.

After the Astros took a 3–0 lead from the first inning, the Mets mustered just two hits against Bob Knepper through eight innings. Dykstra's pinch-hit triple ignited a three-run uprising in the ninth. Roger McDowell, who pitched just once in the first five games of this tight series, threw five innings of one-hit relief in Game 6. In the top of the fourteenth, Wally Backman singled in a run, and the Mets batted for McDowell. In came Messy Jesse.

Dreams of a Scott-free pennant faded when Billy Hatcher homered to left. The game rolled on. In the sixteenth, Ray Knight singled to break the tie, Knight came around on successive wild pitches, Orosco sacrificed (you didn't think he was coming out, did you?), and Dykstra knocked in the third run. That set up the bottom of the sixteenth.

Orosco fanned Craig Reynolds to lead off the inning, his sixth straight batter retired since the home run. Then Davey Lopes walked and Bill Doran singled. Hatcher, representing the tying run, singled to make it 7–5. A force play at second left the Mets one out away from the pennant. Given what happened three days earlier—where the Red Sox rallied to beat the Angels after being down to their last strike in the ALCS—no one was taking anything for granted.

In New York, the city stopped. Bars were packed, and people stood in the street watching soundless TVs through storefront windows as afternoon crawled into night. People with radios were obliged to turn up the volume as people around them—on the subway, in late-working offices, in whatever position superstitious people stand when they want something very badly—moved closer to listen in to the desperate doings at the dome.

Houston cleanup hitter Glenn Davis singled to center, and it was now 7–6; tying run at second, winning run at first, and Kevin Bass at the plate. The Astrodome, where the crowd had been standing for close to five hours, roared so loudly Orosco could barely talk to himself. "You have the ball," the pitcher mumbled. "You still have the power. These guys have given you a cushion, now take advantage of it. Don't blow it."

TRIVIA

Which Mets pitcher was credited with the victory after the ball went through Bill Buckner's legs in Game 6 of the 1986 World Series?

Answers to the trivia questions are on pages 187–189.

After throwing mostly fastballs and getting in trouble, the fatigued southpaw went to his slider. First baseman Keith Hernandez insisted on it during a mound conference. Five straight sliders bent in to Bass, who hit .311 for the season and stepped to the plate batting .304 for the series. With a 3–2 count and the runners moving, the sixth slider was swung on and missed.

The Mets piled out of the dugout to mob the pitcher. The celebration raged in the Astrodome visitor's clubhouse and on the flight all the way back to New York. Phil Pepe, the only *New York Daily News*

TOP 10

Most Career Appearances by Mets Pitchers

Player	Games
1. John Franco	695
2. Tom Seaver	401
3. Jerry Koosman	376
4. Jesse Orosco	372
5. Tug McGraw	361
6. Armando Benitez	333
7. Dwight Gooden	305
8. Jeff Innis	288
9. Turk Wendell	285
10. Roger McDowell	280

writer who picked the Astros to win the series, wrote, "The World Series…can only be an anticlimax." Wrong again.

Orosco wasn't the workhorse in the World Series that he'd been in the Championship Series, pitching four times over eight innings against Houston, winning three games, and fanning 10 (yet Mike Scott was the first player on a losing team to be NLCS MVP). Still, Orosco made four World Series appearances, allowed just two hits, and earned two saves. In Game 4 he came on in the eighth to retire Wade Boggs to end Boston's only threat. Then he set down the Red Sox in the ninth. Orosco's role in epic Game 6 was minor because manager Davey Johnson didn't double-switch when the reliever came in. But Orosco retired his only batter, Bill Buckner, in a game the first baseman would rather blot from the scrolls of time.

Orosco entered Game 7 in the eighth inning after the Mets had rallied and the Red Sox had responded by knocking out McDowell. With New York up 6–5, two runners on, no one out, and Rich Gedman batting, Orosco retired the side with no further damage. Then he got a bat in his hands. The Mets had two men on with one out and Orosco batting. Just as NBC broadcaster Joe Garagiola said he'd bet his house Orosco would sacrifice, the pitcher showed bunt, pulled the bat back, and singled to center on the old "butcher boy" trick to plate the eighth run. "Joe, you just lost your house," retorted broadcasting partner Vin Scully.

Orosco retired Ed Romero and Wade Boggs in the ninth, bringing up Marty Barrett, batting .448 for the Series with 13 hits, five walks, and only one strikeout. If Barrett got on, the heart of the Boston order followed. He worked the count to 2–2, but like Bass in Houston, Barrett missed...and Orosco's glove went airborne.

It seemed like 20 years before it came down. Or at least 17 years. That's how long Orosco played after 1986. He wore nine different uniforms—the Mets traded him after the 1987 season and he spent 2000 spring training as a Met—before he finally decided to retire not long before his 47th birthday. The offers were still coming. He pitched in 1,252 games, more than any man in major league history, but he never saw another World Series. He threw his last pitch as a Twin with the organization that had drafted him in 1978.

It's funny how the Mets southpaw who got the last out in the 1969 World Series was traded for the lefty who got the last out in 1986 for the club's second world championship. Who's Orosco? Indeed.

A Championship Hangover

Dwight Eugene Gooden and Darryl Eugene Strawberry shared more than just a middle name. They were both baseball prodigies whose problems with drugs, alcohol, family, and fame damaged their careers and tarnished their legacies. The two still have bigger concerns than how the public remembers them.

But to Mets fans not completely turned off by the team during its lifeless period in the early 1980s, Strawberry and Gooden represented a chance that maybe the club could reverse its fortunes. Even if the phenoms were on farm teams far away, every time their names came up on a broadcast, it brought some life to the otherwise drab doings at Shea.

As a reward for finishing with the worst record in baseball in 1979, the Mets had the first pick in the amateur draft the next year. Frank Cashen used the first pick of the new regime to take a slugging outfielder from California with an instantly memorable name. Two years later, they used the fifth overall pick—the Mets had improved so much that they were only the fifth-worst team in the game—on a talented Florida pitcher who also had a catchy name. By 1984 the names Strawberry and Gooden followed one another when people talked about the suddenly formidable Mets. The names followed one another on the list of National League Rookies of the Year. The two tall, lean stars, both so strong and successful at such a young age, went down the same path, both good and bad.

By the end of October 1986, Gooden had a career record of 58–19, 744 strikeouts, and an ERA below 2.30, plus a 1985 Cy Young Award, a 1986 World Series ring, and had been chosen to three All-Star teams in three major league seasons. He was beloved in the

By the NUMBERS **23**—The Mets had their biggest offensive day ever in a 23–10 rout at Wrigley Field on August 16, 1987. Greg Maddux, 21, took the loss, and Ron Darling, plagued by bad luck all season, got oodles of support. Darryl Strawberry just missed the cycle, hitting two doubles, a triple, and a home run while scoring five, driving in five, and stealing a base.

media capital and endorsement offers were piling up. Then he missed the '86 victory parade. Then he was pulled over and got into a fight with police in Tampa. Then he failed a urine test two weeks before the '87 season was set to start. Ironically, it was a drug test Gooden had himself inserted into his lucrative contract after his first season. The Mets, with such lofty expectations and dreams of another championship, were left without their Opening Day starter.

By the time Gooden returned to New York on June 5, the defending world champions were in fourth place with a .500 record. Injuries would befall the other four starters from the talented '86 staff, plus rookie David Cone, who was one of the club's most dependable pitchers until he broke his hand trying to bunt in San Francisco. The Mets needed Gooden to help the team retain its swagger and to fill a spot in the rotation. Columnist Dick Young, who a decade earlier with the *Daily News* had provided the final straw to get Tom Seaver out of town, was determined to undermine the best Mets pitcher since Seaver. Young, now with the *New York Post*, told readers to stand up and boo when Gooden made his return. This time no one paid attention to the bitter old man. Gooden beat the Pirates that night and he would lead the decimated pitching staff in victories despite missing 10 starts in drug rehab.

Gooden added stability to a team suffering a year of strange events:

- A lazy fly ball by Dion James at Shea hit a pigeon and dropped for a double on April 12. The Braves slaughtered the Mets.
- Montreal's Tim Raines had to sit out the first month of the season because no other team would sign the All-Star (read: collusion). Rules forbid him to sign with his old club until

DID YOU KNOW . . . That Terry Leach, a reliever and spot starter, began 1987 with a 10–0 record? Forced into the rotation because of injuries to the staff and Dwight Gooden's absence, Leach had the best start to a season in Mets history. He finally lost on August 15, to the Cubs, but finished his finest year at 11–1.

May 1. Without benefit of spring training, he made his first start on NBC's *Game of the Week* and went 4-for-5 against the Mets. He started the game-tying rally in the ninth, and hit a tie-breaking home run in the tenth.

- Backup catcher Barry Lyons, who broke John Tudor's leg while chasing a pop foul in the Cardinals dugout in April, had a bizarre play go against him in June. After doubling to tie the game at Wrigley Field in the ninth inning, he was inexplicably picked off second base during an intentional walk. The Mets lost in the bottom of the ninth.

- Keith Hernandez made two errors in an inning. Hernandez shaved his mustache for the first time since 1978, the year he began his streak of Gold Gloves, and hit two home runs the next day at Wrigley.

- Ron Darling had a no-hitter for seven innings until Greg Gross broke it up with a triple. The Phillies scored three in the eighth and two in the bottom of the ninth to beat the Mets, 5–4.

- Playing every day for the first time as a Met, Howard Johnson exploded. Several managers thought his bat would, too. The league X-rayed his bat for cork. It was clean, but there were plenty of other suspects in a year when home runs increased by 17 percent. HoJo set an NL record with 36 home runs as a switch hitter.

- Despite all the difficulties, the Mets were one and a half games back in September and one out away from a crucial win when Terry Pendleton's two-run homer tied the game in the ninth. The Cardinals won in 10 innings. Earlier, Darling was lost for the year when he tore thumb ligaments diving for a bunt. He had a one-hitter at the time.

Despite everything, the Mets contended until the final week of the 1987 season. It would seem that Strawberry deserved much of the credit. He had his finest season to date, surpassing 30 doubles, 30 homers, 100 RBIs, and just missing 100 walks. He even exceeded 150 games in the outfield for the first time. Strawberry finished sixth in the league MVP voting, but he got scant appreciation from his teammates.

Strawberry's brooding had begun in earnest when Davey Johnson had double-switched him out of Game 6 of the 1986 World Series. His constant tardiness and sick calls led to numerous fines

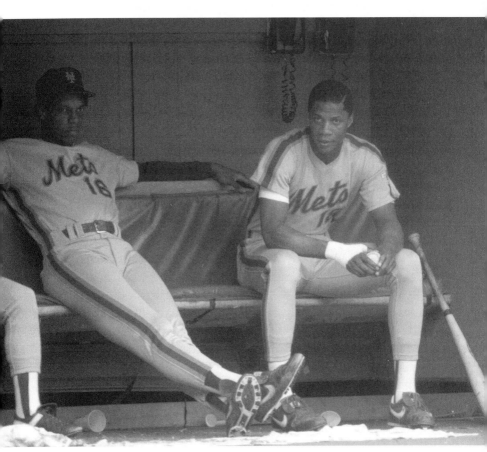

For Dwight Gooden (left) and Darryl Strawberry, the 1986 championship set into motion an almost-tragic turn of events. Photo courtesy of Getty Images.

and angry teammates in '87. At least he gave the new 24-hour sports radio station, WFAN, something to talk about.

Lee Mazzilli, who'd spent years at empty Shea Stadium while Strawberry was still in high school, was disgusted. Maz said Straw was "letting his teammates down." Wally Backman took it a step further: "Nobody I know gets sick 25 times a year," he said.

Backman, who would have his own demons in later years, hit close to home with Strawberry, who called him a "little redneck." No matter how often Strawberry was fined or even benched, he didn't change. He liked being out in the scene and craved all the things that happened in the early hours, especially in the cocaine-crazed 1980s. Yet when he reached the nadir of his Mets career on January 26, 1990, and was arrested for punching his first wife and threatening her with a gun, he would only admit to a problem with alcohol. He spent four weeks at Smithers Alcohol Treatment Center in Manhattan. "Going to Smithers was a cover-up," Strawberry admitted in Michael Sokolove's 2004 book, *The Ticket Out*. "I never even bothered telling them about the drugs."

TRIVIA

Which future Met was taken by the Cubs with the first pick in the 1982 amateur draft, the same draft that saw Dwight Gooden taken with the fifth overall pick?

Answers to the trivia questions are on pages 187–189.

Strawberry was back in his accustomed cleanup spot by Opening Day 1990, and he had perhaps his finest season as a Met. It was also his last year at Shea Stadium. Strawberry's five-year, $20.3 million contract with the Dodgers was a blessing and a curse. Strawberry had always played poorly in Los Angeles while a Met. He only seemed concerned with hitting a mammoth home run every time up, and as a result he batted less than .200 at Dodger Stadium for the Mets. Injuries gave the distracted Strawberry even more time to sit around in Los Angeles. It was with the Dodgers in 1994 that he admitted his addiction to cocaine. Less than a year after going to the Betty Ford Clinic as a Dodger, he failed a drug test as a Giant. He was confined to his spacious home by a judge for tax evasion.

By the NUMBERS — 30–30 Mets

Player	Year	Home Runs	Stolen Bases
Darryl Strawberry	1987	39	36
Howard Johnson	1987	36	32
Howard Johnson	1989	36	41
Howard Johnson	1991	38	30

Johnson and Strawberry were the first teammates in baseball history to have 30 home runs and 30 stolen bases in the same season in 1987.

He played his way back to the big leagues with the independent St. Paul Saints and was rewarded by George Steinbrenner with a Yankees contract. Strawberry was later diagnosed with colon cancer. He had a drug relapse. He spent almost a year in prison for cocaine possession. The trouble he managed to find is prodigious. His baseball numbers seem impressive when compared to players with far less talent. He drove in an even 1,000 runs. He homered 335 times. But his problems—including injuries—may have cost him about 1,000 games over 17 seasons.

"When he wanted to be, he was as good as it gets," Davey Johnson said. "But the thing is, I don't think he was hungry enough to do the 600-home run deal. Darryl is no dummy. He was comfortable hitting 34 home runs a year and stealing 30 bases. He knew what it would take to do more, and he didn't want to do it. He made a calculation. To be one of the real greats, it has to be your whole world, and Darryl had other things going on."

Dwight Gooden's career never reached the heights it seemed destined for, either. He continued to win at a rate that only Mets Tom Seaver and Jerry Koosman had reached before him. Gooden passed Koosman for second on the club's all-time victories list at age 27 in 1992. But he wasn't the same Doc by then. Injuries had caught up with him, and the Mets no longer provided the run support they had always seemed to muster when he took the hill. Still, he

TOP 10

Mets Records Set by Ed Kranepool (1962–1979) and Those Broken by Darryl Strawberry (1983–1990)

1. Games: 1,853
2. At-Bats: 5,436
3. Hits: 1,418
4. Doubles: 225
5. Home Runs: 118 (now held by Darryl Strawberry, 252)
6. Runs Batted In: 614 (now held by Darryl Strawberry, 733)
7. Total Bases: 2,047
8. Extra-Base Hits: 368 (now held by Darryl Strawberry, 469)
9. Pinch Hits: 90
10. Sacrifice Flies: 58

remained a fan favorite and was cut far more slack in all quarters than Straw ever got. Then, just a few weeks before the 1994 strike, Gooden was suspended for failing a drug test. He never again pitched for the Mets.

Like Strawberry, Gooden continued in the major leagues and found a willing benefactor in Steinbrenner. Gooden even threw a no-hitter with the Yankees, but his 194 career wins seemed like so much less than what everyone at Shea felt when the place was packed and Doc was dealing. "In 1985, Dwight Gooden was a real life Sidd Finch," announcer Tim McCarver said, comparing Gooden to George Plimpton's fictitious Mets pitcher who was impossible to hit. Real life intervened and ruined the story.

When the Mets celebrated their 20th anniversary of the 1986 world championship on August 19, 2006, Gooden was the most visible absentee. Davey Johnson and Ray Knight weren't there, either. They had prior commitments. Gooden was in prison. By then he was so addicted to cocaine and had relapsed so many times that he was better off in jail than on the streets.

Strawberry made it for the 20th anniversary celebration and was lauded for his '86 heroics. But why didn't they win in '87? Or the years that followed? Frank Cashen, who drafted the two men, is far enough removed and old enough not to mince words.

"Dwight Gooden and Darryl Strawberry were the guys who really let us down," Cashen told Jeff Pearlman in *The Bad Guys Won!* "Those two men not only let themselves down but the team and the fans of New York. That team was destined to be a dynasty. Maybe I take this too personally, but in my opinion those two men cost us years of success."

A lot of things doomed the Mets, including several moves in the late 1980s by Cashen, but there were only four players on the team from its rise in 1984 to that club's last winning year in 1990: Ron Darling, Sid Fernandez, Strawberry, and Gooden. It's hard to say that Darling and Fernandez could have done much more than they did. Gooden and Strawberry? It's an open question with a painful answer.

Where's Randy?

The Mets still had their swagger in 1988. The club had some different moving parts, most notably Kevin McReynolds, but it was pretty much the same team that had won it all two years earlier. The Mets led for most of the 1988 season, but instead of putting it away early like the '86 club, they put it away late. More sporting.

The Cardinals, as in 1986, weren't a factor. The defending NL champs, devastated from losing another World Series after being one win away from a title, were already seven games out when the Mets arrived in St. Louis in late April. The Pirates were the surprise competition. Pittsburgh had sunk to the bottom of the NL East standings as the Mets had risen during the middle part of the decade. The Bucs had been last in the NL East for three straight years before Jim Leyland's crew won 80 games in 1987. The Pirates would soon become a formidable opponent, but 1988 wasn't their year.

New York's offense was still potent, though it wasn't as good as the prior season. The '87 team had been even better with the bats than the world championship club, setting a home run record that lasted until 2000. The '88 club didn't pine for offense, either, and the pitching was actually better than the '86 edition. The 2.91 ERA was the lowest by the club since the "Year of the Pitcher," now 20 years past. The staff allowed the fewest hits, runs, walks, and homers while striking out more batters than any other team in baseball. The defense committed the fewest errors in the NL in 1988.

Even when the Mets ran into adversity, things worked out. Rick Aguilera, a steady performer at the back end of the rotation for three seasons, went down on April 18 with an arm injury. After going with a four-man rotation for a couple of weeks, Davey Johnson put David

That the Dodgers' home-field advantage in the 1988 NLCS was the result of a football game in Houston in 1986? The Oilers-Bears NFL game at the Astrodome on October 12, 1986, kept the Astros from hosting the three NLCS weekend games in the best-of-seven format. To accommodate the NFL, the National League changed the alternating order rule so the NL West would now have the advantage in even-numbered instead of odd-numbered years. The Mets wound up with weekend games at Shea, and the Astros instead hosted the first two and last two potential games of the series. The '86 Mets won the series dramatically, but the change was felt in '88 when the NL West had the home-field advantage again. The Mets would have hosted Games 6 and 7 against L.A. had the 1986 Oilers played somewhere else that day. By the way, the Bears beat the Oilers, 20–7, in that game.

Cone in the rotation. Cone responded by going 20–3, leading the league in winning percentage, and getting a firm handshake on the field from former President Richard Nixon after his 20th win. Stolen from his hometown Kansas City Royals for Ed Hearn and a fistful of straw in 1987, Cone gave the Mets yet another power arm on a staff with only two pitchers over 30: Terry Leach and Bob Ojeda. Ojeda, coming off an injury-plagued 1987, went just 10–13, but his 2.88 ERA was the lowest of any Mets starter except Cone (2.22).

Half of Ojeda's wins were shutouts, and his strikeouts-to-walks ratio of 4.03 was the best in the league, but the fiery southpaw was also an emotional leader who had helped the Mets push past his former Red Sox teammates in the 1986 World Series. But even as the Mets rolled to a 29–8 finish to run away with the division and reach 100 wins for the third time in history, they did so without their veteran southpaw. As the Mets prepared to clinch the NL East, Ojeda decided to trim a hedge in front of his house. The electric clipper severed the tip of the middle finger on his left hand. He would be out for the postseason, and his career seemed to take a downward spiral from that moment on.

The Mets, though, still had plenty to smile about. They had four solid starters and hard-throwing Randy Myers to finish games—he'd made Jesse Orosco expendable—and call-up Gregg Jefferies was so impressive in 29 games (.321 with six home runs) that he displaced

Howard Johnson. Their NLCS foe was a Dodgers team they'd dominated; New York won 10 of 11 games and outscored them, 49–18. So what if the Dodgers had the home-field advantage?

The Dodgers surprised New York in Game 1, taking a 2–0 lead into the ninth. The Mets scored three times, with Gary Carter driving in the tying and go-ahead runs against Jay Howell. Orel Hershiser, who'd ended the year by setting a major league record with 59 consecutive scoreless innings, had a shutout for eight and one-third innings until Darryl Strawberry doubled to bring in the first run against Hershiser in a month.

Game 2 started late because of a vice presidential debate. After Lloyd Bentsen schooled Dan Quayle, the Dodgers did the same to the Mets. Los Angeles claimed added incentive because of that day's

Kevin McReynolds was one of the key changes from 1986 to 1988. The Mets dominated the season, but this time New York came up just short of the World Series. Photo courtesy of Getty Images.

The NL MVP Candidates in 1998

Player	HR	RBI	AVG	OBP	SLG	SB	Points*
Kirk Gibson	25 (7)	76	.290	.377 (4)	.483 (9)	31	272
Darryl Strawberry	39 (1)	101 (2)	.269	.366 (9)	.545 (1)	29	236
Kevin McReynolds	27 (5)	99 (5)	.288	.336	.496 (6)	21	162

* Points in MVP voting by the baseball writers. League rank in parentheses.

newspaper article bylined by David Cone. Although actually written by reporter Bob Klapisch, who would again elicit the anger of Mets fans with a scathing book in 1993, Cone said that Hershiser was "lucky" and Howell resembled "a high school pitcher." Cone was knocked out after two innings.

New York was quite full of its Mets by the time Game 3 was scheduled to start. The airwaves buzzed with relentless chatter on WFAN, and other stations played the parody of the Randy Newman song "I Love L.A."; at least it was less grating than the tin-eared "Let's Go Mets" song of 1986. A downpour Friday night pushed the game to Saturday, and a college football obligation led NBC to start the playoff game just after noon in a quagmire at Shea. Co-owner Nelson Doubleday was livid, but the Mets endured the frigid afternoon and came away wet but happy.

After Hershiser was removed with the lead, the Mets tallied five times in the eighth. Two of the heroes of 1986, Jesse Orosco and Mookie Wilson, faced each other in a tie game, and Mookie singled in the go-ahead run against the ex-Met. During the uprising, Howell was caught with pine tar on his glove. NL president Bart Giamatti had mercy on him and suspended him just for Game 4. The Dodgers wouldn't use Howell again in the series, but they still had plenty of tricks up their sleeve.

Dwight Gooden and John Tudor were slightly more weather-beaten than the 20-game winners who battled during the fight to the death with the Cardinals in 1985. Gooden was nicked for two

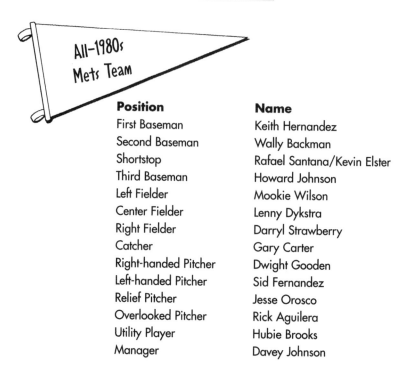

All-1980s Mets Team

Position	Name
First Baseman	Keith Hernandez
Second Baseman	Wally Backman
Shortstop	Rafael Santana/Kevin Elster
Third Baseman	Howard Johnson
Left Fielder	Mookie Wilson
Center Fielder	Lenny Dykstra
Right Fielder	Darryl Strawberry
Catcher	Gary Carter
Right-handed Pitcher	Dwight Gooden
Left-handed Pitcher	Sid Fernandez
Relief Pitcher	Jesse Orosco
Overlooked Pitcher	Rick Aguilera
Utility Player	Hubie Brooks
Manager	Davey Johnson

runs in the first inning of Game 4, but Strawberry and Kevin McReynolds hit back-to-back homers in the fourth. New York knocked out Tudor on Gary Carter's run-scoring triple in the sixth, but a strikeout, a walk, and a double play kept Carter from crossing the plate with the fifth run.

It hardly seemed to matter. Gooden hadn't allowed a hit since the fourth inning. He walked John Shelby to start the ninth, bringing up Mike Scioscia, whom Gooden had retired three times with runners on base. Scioscia, with three home runs all year in 408 at-bats, hit a line drive into the bullpen not far from where closer Randy Myers was warming up. Shea Stadium was so quiet it seemed like 1978 instead of 1988. Three batters later, Myers was in. Mackey Sasser entered as catcher in the double switch. The night shift was in.

The game plodded on through the cold as midnight came and went. Mookie was thrown out stealing by, of course, Scioscia. Scioscia was taken out for Rick Dempsey. Roger McDowell replaced Myers. Kirk Gibson, 1-for-16 in the series to that point, homered in the twelfth. As if the evening hadn't been agonizing enough, the Dodgers used former Mets Tim Leary and Jesse Orosco in the bottom of the twelfth as the Mets loaded the bases. After Orosco got Strawberry to pop up, Hershiser, who'd started two of the first three games, retired McReynolds to end the game.

Some 12 hours later, another game was played amid the stupefying glare of Columbus Day. The Mets sleepwalked through a 7–4 loss and then boarded a plane to Los Angeles for the next night's game (the off day had been absorbed by the rainout). Cone and McReynolds brought life back to the Mets in Game 6. Cone saved a taxed bullpen by tossing a complete game, and McReynolds went 4-for-4 with a home run. The heavily favored Mets were thankful just for a Game 7.

Oh, but for an Ojeda or Aguilera, and maybe a slightly earlier entrance of Myers in Game 4. There was time to think of all this because the deciding game was decided quickly. Darling didn't get an out in the second inning. The clock struck midnight for Jefferies, who booted a bases-loaded grounder by Hershiser that doomed the game. Hershiser mowed down the Mets—again—as the Mets had unthinkably been beaten by the popgun offense of the Dodgers. A team that was next to last in on-base percentage during the year and was one of just five major league teams to hit below 100 homers, had been limited to a .214 average in the playoffs. Yet they won. The parody song "I Hate L.A." was never heard again, but it was felt in the heart of every Mets fan as the Dodgers marched to the world championship. After the hurt had subsided ever so slightly, the Baseball Writers Association announced that Kirk Gibson had been voted NL MVP over Strawberry and McReynolds, whose numbers far surpassed Gibson's.

The expectations had been so high in New York. And whether anyone realized it or not, the brief reign of the Mets was over.

TRIVIA

Which Met made the first and last outs of the first completed night game at Wrigley Field on August 10, 1988?

Answers to the trivia questions are on pages 187–189.

A Distant Second

The Mets finished in second place for the fourth time under Davey Johnson in 1989. Unlike the first three times in the 1980s, when each second-place finish could be interpreted as a pause in the plan or a sacrifice for something greater yet to come, this time it just felt like second place. The Mets just barely held on to second and weren't nearly as close to the NL East–leading Cubs as the final six-game deficit sounded.

Davey Johnson's future was a big story. So was the spring training team photo scuffle between Keith Hernandez and Darryl Strawberry. Straw walked out of camp for a few days and then planted a make-up kiss on Mex for the press. A bigger story still was how Frank Cashen—with plenty of help from assistant Joe McIlvaine—dispatched the players who had made Shea Stadium the most popular place in New York. Wally Backman was sent to Minnesota for three prospects who never prospered. And 1989 quickly turned into a been-at-the-party-too-long summer. The Mets traded three center fielders who manned the same spot in the Shea Stadium outfield for a dozen years: Lee Mazzilli, Mookie Wilson, and Lenny Dykstra. In their place stood Juan Samuel, who would last three months in center field at Shea and was despised by fans.

People respected Samuel's speed and power when he was in Philadelphia, but he'd been converted from second base to center field and it didn't take. With stone-gloved Gregg Jefferies playing second base for the first time, the Mets had two starters playing out of position. Meanwhile, Dykstra and Roger McDowell were now with a division rival. Mazzilli and Wilson went to Toronto a day apart.

DID YOU KNOW . . . That Howard Johnson was the only Met to lead the National League in RBIs through the team's first 44 seasons? HoJo knocked in 117 runs in 1991, breaking Darryl Strawberry's mark of 108 set the previous season. Although HoJo's single-season club RBI mark has since been passed, he remains the only Met to ever lead the league in two Triple Crown categories in one year. In the 1991 NL MVP voting, HoJo, like the Mets, finished fifth.

Dwight Gooden tore a muscle in his shoulder and was essentially done for the year in July. The club needed pitching. At the trading deadline, the Mets brought in Frank Viola, an excellent pitcher at the hitter-loving Metrodome. The deal emptied the farm system—David West was the prominent name, but Kevin Tapani was the one with the goods—and to top it off, Rick Aguilera was included in the five-for-one swap. Aggie was finally over the injuries that had cut his last two seasons short and he had thrived since his conversion to reliever.

When the season was over, the Mets made their biggest move by doing nothing. Keith Hernandez and Gary Carter walked away as free agents. The team co-captains didn't have much left, but the arrival of each earlier in the decade had represented major changes in franchise direction. Hernandez summed up the latest shift before he headed out the door for good. "We don't deserve to win," he said in Chicago during September. "That's the first time I can say that with this team since 1984."

Davey Johnson was retained, although longtime coaches Bill Robinson and Sam Perlozzo were dismissed. The 1990 spring training lockout took some of the glare away from Johnson's situation, but the team's poor start was damning. The deathwatch finally ended with the club at 20–22. The Mets were in fourth place, five and a half games out, although only two National League teams had scored more runs to that point. Players were taking advantage of Johnson's lax style; pitchers and reserves came and went as they pleased from the dugout during games. GM Frank Cashen had to put up with it while the Mets were winning, but now...now they needed a manager, and Cashen tabbed the man who'd done everything the organization had ever asked of him.

In 1991 Howard Johnson led the National League in home runs, RBIs, and errors. Photo courtesy of Getty Images.

Bud Harrelson was a member of the Mets Hall of Fame. (In 1986 Harrelson and Rusty Staub were the first players inducted by the club.) He was a Gold Glove shortstop. He was an All-Star. He was a catalyst in both 1969 and 1973. As Tom Seaver said, "Simply put, we don't win two pennants without him." When he retired, Harrelson hung around Shea Stadium so much that George Bamberger hired him as a coach. The organization asked Harrelson to manage in the low minors. Davey Johnson brought him back to New York to be third-base coach when Bobby Valentine left to manage Texas. Harrelson did all these things well, but one thing he was not equipped to be was a manager in New York.

"What no one could have known was how insecure and paranoid he would be once he sat in the manager's seat," reporters Bob Klapisch and John Harper said of Harrelson in *The Worst Team Money Could Buy.* "The pressures of pennant-race baseball revealed his shortcomings, and as the Mets began to fade, Harrelson was swallowed up by the job."

The team initially took off with a new pilot, but it didn't last. By September 1990 Shea Stadium was littered with strange names. It seems hard to recall the brief Mets tenures of Tom Herr, Pat Tabler, and Dan Schatzeder, but patchwork and glue was all that kept the team in the race. Darryl Strawberry hung in until the end, putting together one of his finest seasons as the only threat in a lineup full of replacements while the Mets tried in vain to overtake the younger, stronger, better-led Pirates. And Strawberry wasn't coming back.

TRIVIA

Which Met made the cover of *Sports Illustrated* after just six at-bats in the major leagues?

Answers to the trivia questions are on pages 187–189.

After Strawberry signed with Los Angeles, the Mets busied themselves with getting rid of yet more names from the glory years: Tim Teufel, Bob Ojeda, and Ron Darling were all gone by midseason 1991, and so was any vestige of competence on the field. Former Cardinals malcontents Garry Templeton and Vince Coleman didn't help. Frank Viola, who'd won 20 games the previous year, whined his "Sweet Music" as the *Titanic* went down. It went down quickly.

The Johnson
Administration

The Starting Lineup for Davey Johnson's First and Last Games As Mets Manager

April 2, 1984 (8–1 loss in Cincinnati)

Wally Backman, Second Base
Jose Oquendo, Shortstop
Keith Hernandez, First Base
George Foster, Left Field
Darryl Strawberry, Right Field
Mookie Wilson, Center Field
Hubie Brooks, Third Base
Ron Hodges, Catcher
Mike Torrez, Pitcher

May 27, 1990 (8–4 loss to San Diego at Shea Stadium)

Gregg Jefferies, Second Base
Kevin Elster, Shortstop
Mike Marshall, First Base
Kevin McReynolds, Left Field
Darryl Strawberry, Right Field
Howard Johnson, Third Base
Daryl Boston, Center Field
Mackey Sasser, Catcher
Dwight Gooden, Pitcher

In April Harrelson quit his own pregame radio show on WFAN with Howie Rose, who grew up idolizing Bud's Mets. Harrelson's inability to handle the infield—something that the old shortstop certainly seemed equipped to do—blew up into the May 24 "Jefferies Fax," a nine-paragraph whimper faxed to WFAN and derided by every media outlet and household in New York. Two weeks later, David Cone ignored Harrelson's call for a pitchout, precipitating a pushing match between manager and pitcher in the dugout; then

Harrelson advised Cone to lie about it to the press. Cone had a rough time of it in July when old pals Strawberry and Carter homered against him as Dodgers.

Yet when Dwight Gooden, one of a handful of remaining '86 vets, beat old pal Ojeda at Shea on July 21, the Mets were 53–38, and just four games out as they departed for the West Coast. Exactly one month later, the Mets were 58–61 and 12½ games behind the Pirates. The Mets had endured the worst road trip in club history, going oh-fer Chicago, St. Louis, and Pittsburgh on a 10-game nightmare. Howard Johnson, having a magnificent offensive season for a dead club, was shifted from third base to shortstop to right field as his 31 errors fit perfectly with his 30 steals and his 38 home runs. (He led the NL in home runs, RBIs, and errors.) A makeup doubleheader with the Expos drew the smallest Shea crowd since 1983, which was fitting because the club had its worst record since '83, the year *before* Davey Johnson took over.

Harrelson was fired with a week to go and Mike Cubbage temporarily took over. Frank Cashen, who'd stayed at the helm too long and had seen his protégé Joe McIlvaine go to San Diego, handed the reigns to Al Harazin. The Mets were now stuck in a mire so thick that any drastic attempt at extrication just spun the wheels and made it that much harder to get out.

Money for Nothing

While the natural reaction is to throw weight off a sinking ship, the 1992 Mets did the opposite. First-year general manager Al Harazin brought in some of the biggest names in the game: Bobby Bonilla, Bret Saberhagen, Willie Randolph, and Eddie Murray joined an existing cast that included Vince Coleman, Howard Johnson, Dave Magadan, David Cone, Sid Fernandez, Dwight Gooden, and John Franco. The Mets also had a few promising players almost ready to emerge from the farm system. They had a new manager in Jeff Torborg, who had awakened the White Sox from a long slumber and yet was allowed to come to the Mets. New York signed Torborg to a four-year, $1.9 million contract. Money was no object.

Bobby Bonilla received $29 million for five years. He had batted in front of Barry Bonds for the Pirates, enjoying all the fastballs such an assignment entailed. Pittsburgh, although a division champion, was under the radar of the national press, and anyone who trekked to Three Rivers Stadium wanted a quote from Barry Bonds. Getting nothing, they settled for a few words from Bobby Bo. The Bronx native understood—or so he thought—the New York media. "I know what you all are gonna try, but you're not gonna wipe this smile off my face," Bonilla said with a grin when he signed with the club. "I grew up in New York. I know what it's all about."

It was about everything other than baseball. Darryl Strawberry's new book said Gooden did drugs during the 1986 season; Gooden, Coleman, and Daryl Boston were accused of rape in Port St. Lucie (the police department later dropped the investigation due to lack of evidence); and three women, known to be Mets groupies, accused Cone of exposing himself to them in the bullpen in 1989. On March

DID YOU KNOW . . . That it took 30 years before the Mets used a position player to pitch in a game? Despite numerous also-ran clubs and blowouts along the way, the first position player to pitch in a game was infielder Bill Pecota, who tossed the eighth inning in a 19–2 loss in Pittsburgh on September 26, 1992. Andy Van Slyke got the only hit off Pecota: a home run.

27 the Mets barred the media—including their own announcers—from the locker room.

The Mets eventually talked, but it wasn't about their crisp play. Bonilla, batting .130 at his new home, was booed with such regularity that he took hitting coach Tom McCraw's advice and wore earplugs to the plate. When a TV camera focused on it, another story was born. Bonilla called to the press box to complain about a scoring decision after he botched a Greg Maddux fly ball in a seven-run first inning. He was further derided as selfish.

On June 4, when the Mets reached Pittsburgh for the first time, the club stood just one game out of first place. In his return to his former home, Bonilla was booed unmercifully and wore a batting helmet in the outfield after a golf ball hit him in the head. In a rare good moment that year, he went 4-for-4 in a 15–1 win at Three Rivers.

The Mets had hoped to challenge a Pirates team with limited resources and the pending exodus of top pitcher Doug Drabek and Barry Bonds for richer environs. When it came to playing baseball, however, the Mets were out of Pittsburgh's league. Except for the one lopsided Mets win, the Pirates won the other six games between the teams in June, including a sweep at Shea with each Pittsburgh win coming by one run.

The Mets had a stretch of 12 losses in 13 games in August, with a surprising Eric Hillman shutout against the Pirates sandwiched between two extra-inning losses. The Pirates clinched their third straight division title during a sweep of the Mets at Three Rivers Stadium in September. Rookie knuckleballer

TRIVIA

Who is the all-time Mets leader in pinch-hit home runs?

Answers to the trivia questions are on pages 187–189.

Tim Wakefield shut out the Mets on the final day of the season for New York's 90th loss of the year, 14 of which came against the Pirates.

The Mets had come apart. Cone, anxious to leave the circus atmosphere, went to Toronto in August for Jeff Kent and Ryan Thompson. Cone finished the year in the World Series; the Mets finished just two games ahead of the last place Phillies.

A book about the disastrous 1992 season, *The Worst Team Money Could Buy*, caused yet more controversy and nearly led to a locker room fight between Bonilla—the smile indeed off his face—and co-author Bob Klapisch. The book's title, however, did not take into account the truth. The '93 season was far, far worse—a straight-to-video sequel to an already bad movie. Their stunts weren't only infantile, they were dangerous. Saberhagen sprayed bleach on a

This unfortunate episode pretty much sums up Bobby Bonilla's tenure in the Big Apple: a fan with the word greed *written on his shirt runs onto the field to throw money at the embattled Met.* Photo courtesy of Getty Images.

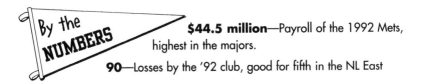

$44.5 million—Payroll of the 1992 Mets, highest in the majors.

90—Losses by the '92 club, good for fifth in the NL East

group of reporters. Coleman clipped an already fragile Gooden with a golf club in the locker room. Coleman threw a firecracker into a crowd and injured a toddler.

Along the way, the Mets fired Jeff Torborg, eating the final two and a half years on his contract. They canned GM Al Harazin. Reliever Anthony Young finally won after a record 27 straight losses; his two-year skid snapped the old mark of 24 set by original Met Roger Craig. The 1993 season was the last in New York for Howard Johnson and Sid Fernandez. They had small roles in the first 100-loss Mets season since 1967, Tom Seaver's rookie year. The 103 losses were the most by the franchise since 1965, Casey Stengel's final season as manager. Even a six-game winning streak to end the season was more a joke than a sign of anything positive. The club finished behind the expansion Florida Marlins, taking a unique place in baseball history by placing seventh in the only season the NL East had that many teams. These Mets did it all.

The Mets had entered the season as the most interesting team in town, a mix of names and personalities that could at least make for good copy. Now the Mets were a joke, no longer worth being covered seriously by the best New York writers or columnists. Their tantrums were worth a day's coverage, but the Yankees were building toward being the main story in town. They hadn't won anything yet, but they were close. The Mets would find getting the attention back from the media and the fans to be harder than rebuilding the team.

Crawling from the Wreckage

Now back with the Mets, general manager Joe McIlvaine had a big mess to try to clean up. He essentially started from scratch, bringing in players from other organizations to put a better team on the field while buying time for the farm system to mature. Rico Brogna, David Segui, Robert Person, and Jose Vizcaino came in trades before the 1994 season. Kevin McReynolds, whose lack of enthusiasm made him unpopular with fans in the 1980s, returned to an initial groan...until fans heard who they'd gotten rid of to get him. Vince Coleman! Just the idea of getting Coleman out of town and bringing back a live body in return made Kevin Mack instantly popular (at least for him). McReynolds was at the end of the line, but Jeff Kent was the club's thumper. The second baseman, as abrasive as McReynolds was impassive, batted .375 in April, including six home runs and 13 RBIs during a five-game home stand. The Mets actually finished the month at 11–11. July was their first month with double-digit wins in '93.

On May 10, 1994, the Mets were four games over .500 and possessor of second place in the new and improved five-team National League East. In first place was the club that interim commissioner Bud Selig had so generously swapped for the Pirates (just as the Bucs stopped being good) in the divisional alignment: the Atlanta Braves. The second-year Marlins were third, followed by the talented Expos, and in the rear came the defending NL champion Phillies. It was a very strange year.

Bret Saberhagen, who'd come to New York for McReynolds and Gregg Jefferies amid great hoopla before the 1992 season, finally showed the ability and maturity that had made him a two-time AL

Cy Young winner and World Series MVP at age 21 in Kansas City. Sabes won 14 games and walked just 13 batters all season. He struck out 11 men for every walk, and he had a Christy Mathewson–like walks-per-nine-innings ratio of 0.66. John Franco led the National League with 30 saves.

The club's payroll of just under $31 million was now in the middle of the NL, and the team's talent level was about the middle of the pack as well. Of course, payroll can be relative. The $19 million

Paul Wilson, tabbed as the leader of Generation K, was, along with Jason Isringhausen and Bill Pulsipher, to be the Mets' mid-1990s answer to Seaver, Koosman, and Matlack of the early 1970s.

By the NUMBERS

Lance A Lot: Hitting Marks Set by Lance Johnson during the 1996 Season

At-Bats: 682 (broken by Jose Reyes in 2005)

Hits: 227 (36 more than Felix Millan's old record)

Triples: 21 (11 more than Mookie Wilson's old mark)

Runs: 117 (now owned by Carlos Beltran with 127 in '06)

Total Bases: 327 (beat out '96 teammate Bernard Gilkey, who had 321)

Expos had the second-lowest payroll in baseball and the most wins of any team when the game was struck down on August 12.

Baseball was spared the indignity of replacement players appearing in regular-season games when the mess was finally settled in April 1995. Despite the bitter taste the strike left in everyone's mouth, the game moved on. That the Mets fell so far behind so early in the shortened 144-game season actually worked to their benefit. There was no pressure to play veterans. The Mets, in fact, dumped their two biggest names in Saberhagen and Bobby Bonilla. Manager Dallas Green held steady with 22-year-old Edgardo Alfonzo, while Rico Bronga played every day and hit 22 home runs, a number that only one Mets first baseman had reached since Dave Kingman's heyday. Catcher Todd Hundley continued making progress with the bat. Carl Everett, picked up from Florida, showed promise in the outfield. Everett's emergence came at the expense of Jeromy Burnitz, a talented slugger who got on Dallas Green's bad side and found himself in Cleveland. Petulant Everett would get into Green's doghouse soon enough.

Bobby Jones emerged as a reliable starter and the team workhorse. Dave Mlicki, who arrived in the Burnitz trade, showed the Mets that he indeed had "stuff" by winning four of his first five decisions. The real arms, though, were down on the farm, and the Mets, miles behind the Braves, saw no harm in bringing them to New York. Bill Pulsipher arrived in June and worked to a 3.98 ERA. Jason

Isringhausen, a 44th-round draft pick in 1991, debuted on July 17 in front of scores of family and friends at Wrigley Field. He pitched a two-hitter for seven innings. Izzy finished his major league apprenticeship at 9–2 (not counting his debut or the season finale, both of which the Mets won after he left). He compiled a 2.81 ERA and finished fourth in the Rookie of the Year voting despite just 14 starts. It was the other outings he made that year, though, that would be brought up in the years to come. He won 20 games at three different levels, starting 32 times over 221 innings all told in Binghamton, Norfolk, and New York. No pitcher in the National League made that many starts or threw as many innings.

Spring training 1996 was full of hype and optimism. The club's six-game winning streak to close the '95 season had vaulted them into a second-place tie, even though they were still six games under .500 and 21 games behind Atlanta. Cuban defector Rey Ordoñez surprised everyone in camp with his remarkable glove (and his puny bat). Paul Wilson, the first pick in the draft just two years earlier, was the media's selected ringleader of "Generation K." Wilson, Pulsipher, and Isringhausen were dubbed the next version of Seaver, Koosman, and Matlack, maybe even better.

"People thought we were the second coming up in New York," Isringhausen recalled. "We had the talent to do it but we all got hurt, basically at the same time."

After just a few weeks of heady articles prophesizing the three of them conquering New York together, Pulsipher went down. Wilson made it into September, and Isringhausen's problems really didn't get started until 1997. In all, they went 14–33 as Mets after 1995. Their failure in New York symbolized what went wrong with the 1996 team. For one of the few times in Shea Stadium history, the team crushed the ball but couldn't get people out.

The Mets tied with Atlanta for second in the National League in batting at .270. Although the Rockies dominated the offensive leaderboard, per usual, the Mets led the NL in triples for the first time in club history. The Mets also set club records for at-bats, hits,

TRIVIA

Which Met was ejected from a game on a day honoring him in 1996?

Answers to the trivia questions are on pages 187–189.

DID YOU KNOW . . . That Derek Wallace was the first—and so far, the only—Met to strike out four batters in an inning? He did it in the ninth inning against the Braves on Friday the 13th in September 1996. Terry Pendleton fanned but reached on a passed ball to start the inning. Wallace whiffed Chipper Jones and allowed a double to Fred McGriff to put the tying runs in scoring position. Wallace then struck out Ryan Klesko and Mike Mordecai for the save.

and average. Scoring and patience proved to be problems, though. The Mets were 10th in both runs and on-base percentage. Todd Hundley's 41 homers broke Roy Campanella's record for most home runs by a catcher and also set the franchise record. Bernard Gilkey, acquired from the Cardinals, set club records for doubles and RBIs. Lance Johnson, signed as a free agent from the White Sox in 1996, would have one of the greatest offensive outputs in club history in his only full season as a Met.

The pitching, though, gave it all back in a frustrating 71–91 campaign. The club's 4.22 ERA was the highest since the inaugural year of Shea Stadium. The staff allowed more runs and walked almost 100 more batters than the brutal 103-loss club of '93. The 159 home runs surrendered were the most by the club in 30 years. Dallas Green, a former pitcher who had already done the impossible twice—bringing a world championship to the Phillies as a manager and building the Cubs into a division winner as a GM—was overmatched in his fourth season at Shea. After he questioned whether the club's young pitchers should even be in the majors, Green was out of a job.

His replacement, Bobby Valentine, was met with a yawn and a shrug as the city's attention focused on the Yankees. With "Generation K" having turned into "Generation DL," fans were weary of rebuilding that never seemed to build anything lasting.

The Winning Team

The Mets' renaissance began with their worst inning in 28 years. After an 11-run sixth on Opening Day in San Diego, starter Pete Harnisch did not pitch again for four months due to depression. The Giants then swept the Mets to start the Shea portion of the schedule in the New York return of Jeff Kent, who'd been traded the previous summer for Carlos Baerga. Baerga was an All-Star on the way down while Kent was ascending to an elite level. His eighth-inning home run dropped the Mets to 3–9. The 1997 Mets looked last-place caliber.

The first baseman, John Olerud, had been so expendable that Toronto sent $5 million American dollars to the Mets to take him. Effective starter Rick Reed had been a replacement player two years earlier, causing animosity with union hard-liners like John Franco. None of the three big bats from '96, Lance Johnson, Bernard Gilkey, or Todd Hundley, would produce those numbers again. Hundley came closest to matching his '96 totals, but he bristled when manager Bobby Valentine suggested he needed more sleep and fewer nights out on the town.

With a $35 million payroll—less than Florida and Cincinnati and only half that of the Yankees—the Mets won 17 more games while batting eight points lower than the previous edition. Valentine and pitching coach Bob Apodaca forged a no-name staff that rarely missed bats (13th in the NL in strikeouts) yet still allowed 70 fewer runs than the previous year. Bobby Jones reeled off 11 wins by early June while free agents Brian Bohanon and Armando Reynoso pitched well. There was scant help from the farm, with only two wins coming from the club's three ballyhooed pitching prospects. New York even got production from mercurial Carl Everett, whose anger

The arrival of Mike Piazza instantly created a buzz in Shea Stadium that had been absent for the previous decade.

IF ONLY . . . The Mets had won one of their last five games in 1998. The Mets lost twice at Shea to an Expos team trying to avoid 100 losses. Then the Mets went to Atlanta and dropped three straight. The Giants, meanwhile, won six of seven and forced a one-game playoff with the Cubs, who went 1–3 to end the season. Chicago captured the wild card playoff behind Steve Trachsel.

overflowed when a domestic problem became public. The free-swinging and stone-gloved Butch Huskey moved around the field enough to collect 24 home runs and 81 RBIs. Valentine created a solid bench out of unwanted players like Matt Franco, Luis Lopez, and Todd Pratt.

Yet the front office was in flux. GM Joe McIlvaine was replaced by Steve Phillips, who spent several weeks working on his first deal: a six-player swap that netted Turk Wendell, Brian McRae, and, regrettably, Mel Rojas from the Cubs (Manny Alexander and unhappy campers Lance Johnson and Mark Clark went to Chicago). There would be many more deals—including the arrival of Al Leiter and Dennis Cook from Florida and Masato Yoshii from Japan in 1998—but the biggest trade Phillips ever made landed a superstar who played the same position as his top slugger.

Todd Hundley was out the first three months of the '98 season with a knee injury. Phillips used quantity to cover up the lack of quality. Tim Spehr, a career .198 hitter, was the Opening Day catcher. By May they'd also used Alberto Castillo, who drove in the only run in the Opening Day marathon; Jim Tatum; Rick Wilkins; and Todd Pratt, who'd inexplicably begun the year in the minors after a solid 1997 season. The Mets remained almost even with Chicago and San Francisco for the wild card, heading into Memorial Day weekend. Shea Stadium, however, was dead.

When the Yankees were forced to play a day game at Shea because a concrete slab fell in the Bronx, the Yankees drew almost 25,000 more than the Mets that night. When Mike Piazza became available, Phillips initially said the Mets weren't interested; they already had a catcher. Word came from the owner's box, from Nelson Doubleday, specifically: get the superstar first and figure out what to do with Hundley later.

That the announcement that Jackie Robinson's No. 42 would be retired throughout baseball was made at Shea Stadium? Commissioner Bud Selig made the decree during the fifth-inning ceremony in the Mets–Dodgers game on April 15, 1997, the 50th anniversary of Robinson's landmark debut in Brooklyn. President Bill Clinton and Rachel Robinson also spoke at Shea that night in front of a full house. Butch Huskey, who wore No. 42, would be allowed to keep the number. Mo Vaughn later wore that number as a Met under the same grandfathered rule.

Piazza arrived to the type of attention that Shea hadn't seen in a decade. He doubled and caught Leiter's shutout in his Mets debut. When Hundley came back, the Mets tried him in left field. No Hundley, neither Todd nor his father, Randy, had ever played a position other than catcher in 1,769 career games. In a situation not unlike the one Piazza would face at first base in 2004, Todd Hundley found plenty of trouble at his new position. Hundley became a backup to the best-hitting catcher in the game. Yet when the season ended, it seemed like Piazza would be the one to leave. The people who filled the previously empty seats at Shea weren't satisfied with a superstar who wound up hitting .348 with 23 homers, 76 RBIs, and a .607 slugging percentage in 109 games as a Met. The boos eventually, rightfully, faded, and Piazza signed a seven-year deal worth $91 million. The Mets may have lost their last five games of the season to miss out on the wild card, but they did lock up the greatest hitter to don a Mets uniform. They also re-signed Leiter and brought in a third baseman from the White Sox who not only gave the Mets the best infield in club history, he made *Sports Illustrated* wonder whether the Mets had the best infield ever.

Robin Ventura and Olerud, who had set the club record by hitting .354 in 1998, gave the Mets two solid left-handed hitters to bookend Piazza. Ventura became the first player in major league history to hit grand slams in both ends of a doubleheader on May 20, 1999. And, of course, there was the defense. "On the left side of the infield Ventura and Ordoñez cover the most ground since Lewis and Clark," *SI* baseball writer Tom Verducci said. Both players won Gold Gloves in 1999, while the low-key but high-yield right side of Olerud and Edgardo Alfonzo went overlooked. Alfonzo, who moved back to second base to accommodate Ventura, did not commit a fielding error all year; his five errors were all on throws. The team set a record with only 20 unearned runs allowed. "What's really impressive is that they don't even play on a great field at Shea," explained Giants first baseman J.T. Snow, who beat out Olerud for the Gold Glove. "They exemplify that strength up the middle wins championships. It's hard to get four guys like that on one infield, and that's why they're going to make the playoffs. Their defense won't break down."

The *offense* is what conked out. The Mets had a four-game lead in the wild card standings with 12 games remaining and had an outside shot at first place in the NL East when they were swept in Atlanta. That was nothing new, but then the Mets were swept in Philadelphia, too. The Mets lost eight of nine at the worst possible time and found themselves two games behind the Reds with three games to play. While the Reds lost consecutive games in Milwaukee, the Mets twice beat Pittsburgh. Houston, which had been tied for first with Cincinnati in the NL Central on the final weekend, eventually won the division. As the Reds waited out a five-hour, 45-minute rain delay in Milwaukee on the final day of the year, Pirates rookie Kris Benson confounded the Mets.

Pittsburgh nicked Orel Hershiser for a run in the first inning. Late-season pickup Darryl Hamilton tied it in the fourth when his line drive landed just fair. With the game still tied and the bases full with one out in the ninth, the Pirates summoned former Met Brad Clontz to face Piazza. The memory of the nightmare ending of 1998 and the presence of the worn-out Piazza, who'd bounced into a league-high 27 double plays, made the mild October afternoon crackle with anticipation and angst. The first pitch skipped to the backstop...and Melvin Mora crossed home plate. The Mets would live for another day.

TRIVIA

The Mets momentarily had their hands on three All-Star catchers on December 1, 1998. Who were they?

Answers to the trivia questions are on pages 187–189.

Leiter, Pratt, and the Grand-Slam Single

One game. The previous 11 October-free seasons boiled down to a single contest, the 163rd game of 1999. An earlier coin flip gave Cincinnati the right to host a one-game wild-card playoff, just the 10th tiebreaker in major league history. No Mets fan stayed late at work that Monday; the anxiety of 1998's failure and the collapse in the final two weeks in '99 all rode on Al Leiter's left arm.

Leiter had allowed nearly twice as many runs as in his dominant first season with the Mets, but he was still the ace. And it was his turn in the rotation. The Reds, who'd waded through ankle-deep water in Milwaukee just to qualify for this game, had 11–3 Steve Parris. Leiter was brilliant, pitching his only complete game of the year and allowing just two hits. The Mets had that many hits two batters into the game. Rickey Henderson, who defied age and the critics by hitting .315 with 37 steals at age 40, singled while the capacity crowd at Cinergy Field settled into their seats. Edgardo Alfonzo followed with a two-run homer. The Mets later tacked on three more runs to let fans in New York breathe. The wait was over.

The laundry was still soaked with champagne when the Mets hit Phoenix the next night for the Division Series. An early lead was gone, and the Mets had the bases loaded in a tie game with one out in the top of the ninth. Matt Williams made a diving stop and recorded the force out at home. Two down. Up stepped Alfonzo. He launched a grand slam, his second home run of the game, and the Mets had their first postseason win since 1988.

The teams split the next two games with the Mets hosting Game 4 on a balmy afternoon at Shea. The Mets held an eighth-inning lead, 2–1, thanks to another Alfonzo homer and a Benny Agbayani double.

With two outs and a man on, Tony Womack smacked a hard grounder to second that somehow eluded Alfonzo. It was ruled a hit, and the Diamondbacks had two men on. Armando Benitez, in the first of many Mets meltdowns at the worst possible moment, surrendered a two-run double to Jay Bell. Melvin Mora, a defensive replacement for Henderson in left field, gunned down Bell trying to score on a single by Matt Williams.

In one of several questionable moves by Buck Showalter in the late innings (another was double-switching Lenny Harris for MVP-candidate and four-time Gold Glove third baseman Matt Williams), Tony Womack moved from shortstop to right field and Gregg Olson entered to pitch the eighth. Olson walked Alfonzo to start the inning. Lefty Greg Swindell came in and induced John Olerud to hit a high fly to right. Womack dropped it as Shea exploded. Roger Cedeño, who

Unlikely hero Todd Pratt (No. 7) homered in the tenth inning of Game 4 of the 1999 NLDS to give the Mets their first postseason series win since 1986.

Home Runs in Mets History

1. **Todd Pratt** (October 9, 1999): Everyone watching, including Steve Finley, assumed the ball was caught in the tenth inning of Game 4 of the NLDS. Not so. It's the only series-ending postseason home run in franchise history and forever crowned Pratt as the greatest backup catcher in Metdom.

2. **Lenny Dykstra** (October 11, 1986): The 13 years between postseason games at Shea felt like an eternity. In Game 3, the favored Mets trailed in the ninth inning when Dykstra, who didn't even start the game, smacked a ball into the bullpen to beat Dave Smith and the Astros. It made it almost worth the wait between Shea Octobers.

3. **Donn Clendenon** (October 16, 1969): Moments after the Cleon Jones shoe-polish incident, Clendenon's blast to left off Dave McNally put the Mets back in Game 5 of the 1969 World Series. The Mets were down, 3–0, until the third homer of the Series by Clendenon, a midseason pickup from the expansion Expos. The Mets didn't trail for long.

4. **Al Weis** (October 16, 1969): An inning after Clendenon's blast, Weis homered to tie Game 5 in the seventh. He hit just two home runs all season, and the Mets scored twice in the eighth and won one of the most unlikely world championships in the game's history.

5. **Ray Knight** (October 27, 1986): Just like the inevitable 1969 miracle, the Game 6 magic and the Game 7 comeback made victory in 1986 seem like a question of *when*, not *if*. Knight was the who in the when. His seventh-inning home run snapped a 3–3 tie and gave the Mets the lead they never relinquished.

6. **Lenny Dykstra** (October 21, 1986): For a guy who hit just 34 home runs as a Met (postseason included), Dykstra hit a couple of huge ones. Losing the first two games of the World Series at home to Boston had substantially dented

the Mets' bravado; Nails started Game 3 with a home run, and the Mets went up 4–0 in the first. The first two games became mulligans after Dykstra's drive at Fenway.

7. **Mike Piazza** (September 21, 2001): In the first outdoor sporting event held in New York after the 2001 World Trade Center tragedy, Mike Piazza came up with the Mets down 2–1 in the eighth inning and crushed a ball against Atlanta's Steve Karsay. It gave the surging Mets the lead and momentarily took some people's minds off far, far weightier issues. It still brings goose bumps to see the replay. Terry Cashman even wrote a song about the blast.

8. **Benny Agbayani** (October 7, 2000): In the bottom of the thirteenth inning, with a stiff wind blowing in, Benny Agbayani mashed an Aaron Fultz pitch into the picnic area to give the Mets a two games to one lead over the Giants in the NLDS. It was the second straight game the underdog Mets won in extra innings against San Francisco.

9. **Darryl Strawberry** (October 1, 1985): The guy could hit the ball a long way, but his most memorable shot came in the eleventh inning against the Cardinals in a do-or-die series opener in 1985. Straw's long blast off the Busch Stadium scoreboard clock was the only run of the game.

10. **Dave Kingman** (April 14, 1976): It was windy—it was, after all, Chicago—but Kong's gargantuan blast of more than 530 feet bounced off the third house down Waveland Avenue. Kingman piled up homers like no Met before him during those first three months of '76, and he did it with an on-field panache (off-field was a whole different ballgame) that almost made one forget the previous winter's catastrophic Rusty Staub–Mickey Lolich deal.

had—believe it or not—entered the game in the top of the inning as a defensive replacement, tied the game with a sacrifice fly. With disturbing visions of Randy Johnson pitching the next night in Arizona, the game moved on.

Matt Mantei held the Mets hitless for two innings, getting Todd Pratt to ground out with the bases loaded. Pratt, 0-for-7 in the series, was playing because of a painful thumb injury that kept Mike Piazza from starting either game at Shea. Mantei, who'd cost Arizona two prospects in midseason, including Brad Penny, had saved 22 games in three months for the 100-win Diamondbacks. Pratt slammed a line drive to dead center, and Steve Finley, who would win his third Gold Glove in 1999, quickly tracked the ball to the base of the wall.

"It should have been an easy catch," Finley said. "I didn't jump high enough, and the ball hit off the top of my glove.... I thought I had it. I felt it in my glove. It took me a second to realize I didn't catch it. I still don't believe it."

Neither could Pratt. "I wanted to cry," he said of the moment when Finley slapped his glove and put his hands on his hips. It was just the fourth series-ending home run in postseason history. "Two celebrations in one week after waiting my whole career for one," winning pitcher John Franco said in the soaked clubhouse.

The killjoy Braves wrapped up the other NLDS and turned off the lights in the Astrodome. The same team that had beaten the Mets five times in six games in the closing weeks of the season—and had a 9–3 mark against the Mets during the year—was ready to spoil the party.

The Braves took the first three games with Greg Maddux and Tom Glavine pitching gems and John Smoltz coming out of the bullpen for the first time—and certainly not the last time—to save the middle game. The Mets held a 1–0 lead in the eighth inning of Game 4, but tiring starter Rick Reed surrendered consecutive home runs to Brian Jordan and Ryan Klesko. Smoltz pitched superbly (as a starter this time) into the bottom of the eighth. After Mike Remlinger struck out his only batter, Bobby Cox pulled a double-switch: Ozzie Guillen came in to play short and John Rocker took the mound. Rocker, who'd later stick his foot in his mouth with his infamous diatribe on

IF ONLY ... John Franco and Armando Benitez hadn't both blown saves in Game 6 of the 1999 NLCS. A victory would have forced Game 7 and put all the pressure on the Braves, who had led the series, three games to none. No other team facing a four-game sweep had ever forced a seventh game. It would at least have been fun to watch.

All-1990s
Mets Team

Position	Name
First Baseman	John Olerud
Second Baseman	Edgardo Alfonzo
Shortstop	Jose Vizcaino
Third Baseman	Robin Ventura
Left Fielder	Bernard Gilkey
Center Fielder	Lance Johnson
Right Fielder	Jeromy Burnitz/Carl Everett
Catcher	Mike Piazza
Right-handed Pitcher	Bobby Jones
Left-handed Pitcher	Al Leiter
Relief Pitcher	John Franco
Overlooked Pitcher	Rick Reed
Utility Player	Matt Franco
Manager	Bobby Valentine

New Yorkers and the number seven train in *Sports Illustrated*, issued a walk and was victimized by a double steal by Cedeño and Mora. Olerud hit a bouncer up the middle past the no-longer-so-agile Guillen. Both runs scored, and the Mets had the lead. Guillen just missed a home run in the top of the ninth and Benitez set down the side. The Mets would live for another day, and what a day it would be.

John Olerud homered against Greg Maddux in the first inning for a 2–0 lead in Game 5. Masato Yoshii pitched well for three innings, but three straight hits in the fourth tied the game and brought in Orel Hershiser, the first of eight relievers used by Bobby Valentine. After that, the Bobby versus Bobby chess match grew in complexity as a mist changed into steady rain. The tarp never budged.

By the fifteenth inning, the Braves had seen two runners tagged out at the plate and had nearly run out of players, but they took the lead on a triple by Keith Lockhart against Octavio Dotel. Rookie Kevin McGlinchy battled Shawon Dunston in an epic 12-pitch at-bat before the veteran singled to center. Pinch hitter Matt Franco

TRIVIA

Which Met threw the last
two pitches of an
intentional walk, and
then was promptly
removed in Game 5 of
the 1999 NLCS?

Answers to the trivia questions are on pages 187–189.

walked, and Alfonzo bunted the runners over. Olerud was walked intentionally, and Pratt, playing the hero once more, walked to tie the game. With the infield and outfield in, Robin Ventura, who'd been hitless in the series until the eleventh inning, clubbed a ball that somehow cleared the wall in right. Five hours, 46 minutes later, the game was over, 7–3. Not exactly. Pratt was so over-joyed he tackled Ventura after he rounded first base. Umpires called Pratt out for passing the runner, nullifying the other runs. The Mets still won, 4–3, but Ventura's hit went from home run to single—not just any single, "the Grand-Slam Single."

Two days after using 44 players, including a postseason-record 15 pitchers, the two clubs battled past midnight in Atlanta. New York trailed 5–0 in the first, 7–3 in the sixth, tied it in the seventh on Piazza's dramatic home run, took the lead in the top of the eighth, blew it in the bottom of the eighth, took the lead in the tenth, and blew it in the bottom of the tenth. After the Mets went down in the eleventh, Gerald Williams doubled and the Braves bunted him to third. Valentine ordered consecutive intentional walks to set up a force at any base. Kenny Rogers, who'd once pitched a perfect game, walked Andruw Jones to bring in the winning run.

Thank you for coming. Please step away from the ride.

Building on Success

No Mets club had ever reached the postseason two years in a row. General manager Steve Phillips not only wanted to achieve that goal, he wanted to take the pennant. It wouldn't be easy. All roads led through Atlanta, and there were also several other top National League clubs. Never one to sit still, Phillips brought in free agent Todd Zeile to play first base after John Olerud signed with his hometown Mariners. The centerpiece of this "go for it now" mantra came just before Christmas 1999, when Phillips acquired Mike Hampton (plus big-dollar, free-spirit, Derek Bell) for outfielder Roger Cedeño and hard-throwing rookie Octavio Dotel. Hampton was coming off a 22-win season and his sinker figured to thrive at spacious Shea.

"This was the one thing we lacked," Phillips said. "We wanted to add a guy like that to our starting pitching, that you could pitch at the front end of a series. That was very important to us." The presence of Hampton and Al Leiter at the top of the rotation was something few teams could match. The 2000 Mets finished third in the league in ERA (4.16) and allowed the lowest opponents' average in baseball (.252).

The season began at sunrise New York time, with the first-ever regular-season games from Japan. Mike Hampton was wild in his debut, and WFAN provided a baseball first: a postgame show in morning drive time. Benny Agbayani, brought to the Far East only because the Mets didn't need a full complement of pitchers, hit a grand slam against the Cubs in the eleventh inning of the second game to salvage Tokyo.

Back in the U.S., the Mets reeled off a nine-game April winning streak. Then they gave it back with an ugly 13-game road trip. When

Although losing the 2000 Series to the Yankees was a bitter disappointment, Mets fans took some consolation in the complete unraveling of Roger Clemens in front of the entire viewing world. Photo courtesy of Getty Images.

Rickey Henderson only reached first on a ball off the wall—he assumed it was a home run—Rickey was released, Joe McEwing was recalled, and the Mets started their mix-and-match outfield parade. For a club with 16 players making at least $2 million per year, the club's three best outfielders—Melvin Mora, Jay Payton, and Agbayani—made $645,000 all told. Veteran Darryl Hamilton had toe problems, and Derek Bell was, well, Derek Bell. He marched to his own drummer (presumably on the stereo system on his plush houseboat), far removed from the role of "Killer B" he'd assumed in Houston.

The Mets moved the versatile Mora to shortstop after Rey Ordoñez broke his arm in May. Spoiled by Ordoñez's defense, the Mets pined for a better glove to fit their championship aspirations. Mora's error on a sure double play ball cost the Mets a game in Boston. A couple of weeks later, just before the trading deadline, the Mets picked up Orioles shortstop Mike Bordick for Mora plus three other young players. The verdict? Mora made seven errors in 44 games, displaying slightly below average range. Bordick had seven errors in 56 games with slightly below average range, and he was hurt when the Mets needed him most. The same day Bordick was acquired, the Mets sent former first-round picks Paul Wilson and Jason Tyner to Tampa Bay for an outfielder and a reliever.

TRIVIA

What was the name of the 2000 film with a plot that revolved around the 1969 Mets?

Answers to the trivia questions are on pages 187–189.

The three newcomers certainly had good starts. Bordick and Bubba Trammell hit home runs in their first at-bats as Mets; Rick White earned a relief win in his debut. Timo Perez got a hit in his first Mets at-bat on September 1, and he never stopped hitting. The Mets experienced their annual September skid earlier than usual, and Timo helped them pull out of it and capture the wild card again. On a team without much speed—they stole 84 fewer bases than in 1999—Timo was an ideal leadoff hitter. When Derek Bell was injured at Pac Bell in the Division Series opening loss, Bobby Valentine quickly inserted Timo in the lineup. He started a dozen postseason games in a row, batting .294 in the Division Series and .304 in the NLCS, before faltering in the World Series.

It was the lesser-known names that proved to be the heroes against the Giants. Although All-Star Al Leiter left with a three-run lead in the ninth inning in Game 2 in San Francisco, Armando Benitez surrendered a three-run homer to pinch hitter J.T. Snow. After the first two Mets went down in the tenth, pinch hitter Darryl Hamilton doubled against Felix Rodriguez. Payton then singled in the go-ahead run. John Franco struck out Barry Bonds to save it for Benitez.

The Mets no-names kept coming up big. Benny Agbayani homered into a gusty wind in the thirteenth inning to win Game 3. Veteran Bobby Jones clinched the series with a one-hitter. Jeff Kent had the only hit, but the Giants had Jones in trouble in the fifth inning. Because he'd worn through his bullpen the previous day, Dusty Baker let pitcher Mark Gardner bat with two outs and the bases loaded. He popped up to strand the only base runners the Giants had all game.

The Cardinals handled the chore of sweeping the Braves, but the Mets did them no favors in the Championship Series. Hampton was masterful in his two starts, shutting out the Cardinals over 16 innings and fanning 12 to earn MVP.

New York won Game 2 in St. Louis on two errors in the ninth. After dropping Game 3 at Shea, the Mets pounded five doubles in the first inning of Game 4 and cruised to the win. Todd Zeile's bases-clearing double literally made the stadium shake in Game 5; Timo Perez looked like he was still swaying in the ninth as he jumped up to catch the final out. Just like that, the Mets were in the World Series. It looked so easy that it was hard to figure out why it had taken 14 years.

By the NUMBERS

10—Runs scored in the eighth inning on June 30, 2000, overcoming an 8–1 deficit to the Braves. It not only tied a 1979 club record (broken in 2006), but it ignited the huge crowd that had stuck around on Fireworks Night. Edgardo Alfonzo got the game-tying hit, and Mike Piazza's line-drive three-run home run put the Mets ahead, 11–8. John Rocker, subject to his own security for his remarks about New York, was conspicuously absent.

DID YOU KNOW . . . Al Leiter and Tom Seaver each started seven postseason games as Mets? Of course, Seaver did not have the Division Series to boost his total. Seaver went 3–3; Leiter was 0–2, but Armando Benitez blew two wins.

These heady thoughts dissipated quickly with the Subway Series. Something many New Yorkers had waited their whole lives to see became a spectacle Mets fans needed to shield their eyes from. Benitez blew Game 1, and the Mets lost in 12. A late comeback fell short the next night, a mere sideshow to the Roger Clemens–Mike Piazza theatrics. The Mets managed to win back Shea Stadium, half-filled with Yankees fans, on a deciding Agbayani double off Orlando Hernandez in Game 3. That ended the Yankees' 14-game winning streak in the World Series. A moral victory? Big deal.

The Yankees took the next two games, beating Al Leiter in the game of his life, with Luis Sojo hitting his 142nd pitch up the middle on 142 hops to drive in the go-ahead run in the top of the ninth. Piazza's deep liner died in the wind and so did a piece of every Mets fan. A great season was reduced to ashes; a pennant winner became just a loser in its hometown. No one could have thought it, but this low moment would be the high point for a few years to come.

Mikey P. and Bobby V.

Mike Piazza and Bobby Valentine were a couple of Northeast guys who came up with the Dodgers a generation apart. Valentine was a heralded prospect who got hurt, and Piazza was a 62nd-round draft pick who became a star when given the chance. Both traveled many miles to a dilapidated building and helped it rock like it was 1999. It was.

The Mets had spent big. In 1998 they'd traded for and then signed both Piazza and Al Leiter. Then, free agent Robin Ventura came to play third, a position shift gave the infield a solid right side with John Olerud and Edgardo Alfonzo, and the bullpen was as good as it had been in years with Turk Wendell slamming the rosin bag, Armando Benitez firing bullets, and John Franco cleaning up the rest. So why were the Mets losing? Heading into Memorial Day weekend, the Mets had been 27–20, one and a half games out of first place in the NL East; eight game and eight losses later they stood in third place in the division with seven teams in front of them for the wild card. Coaches Bob Apodaca, Tom Robson, and Randy Niemann were fired. Valentine read about Apodaca, his trusted pitching coach, in the newspaper before leaving for a game at Yankee Stadium; he found out about the others when he arrived in the Bronx. Valentine almost quit, but he told general manager Steve Phillips he would resign if the team struggled over the next 55 games. He liked to be specific.

How did the team react? The Mets went 40–15 over the next third of the season. Not bad for morons. That's pretty much what Valentine called several players in a *Sports Illustrated* article at the end of the season. "You're not dealing with real professionals in the clubhouse. You're not dealing with real intelligent guys for the most

TOP 10

Most Games Caught by a Met

1.	Jerry Grote	1,176
2.	Mike Piazza	827
3.	Todd Hundley	745
4.	John Stearns	678
5.	Gary Carter	566
6.	Ron Hodges	445
7.	Duffy Dyer	326
8.	Mackey Sasser	261
9.	Vance Wilson	255
10.	Chris Cannizzaro	236

part," Valentine said of a players-only clubhouse meeting during a season-threatening losing streak in Philadelphia. "Because there's about five guys in there right now who are losers, who are seeing if they can recruit." And this from a manager who'd been suspended for wearing a disguise—and a bad one at that—in the dugout following an ejection.

With the memory of the five straight season-ending losses that had doomed the 1998 season hanging over the club, Valentine's club regrouped. The Mets won a one-game playoff in Cincinnati on a gem by Al Leiter, whose victory at Yankee Stadium had jump-started that critical 55-game segment. "Bobby makes things easier for the players," Leiter said. "He knows when he's needed and he becomes a lightning rod."

Mike Piazza proved more a leader by example. He let his bat talk for him on the field. The game's greatest hitting catcher, however, was just as proud of catching a shutout as he was of going 4-for-4. The fans knew they were getting everything he had. Hence the five-minute standing ovations at the end of his Mets career and during his return in a Padres uniform in 2006. "Mike P-I-A-Z-Z-A," the crowd thundered over and over again.

Piazza was a magnet for every foul tip, every wild swing, every home plate collision, yet he was one of most durable catchers in

Even when some of his teammates seemed to be lacking, Mike Piazza proved to be one of the classiest players to wear a Mets uniform. Here he is shown honoreing the fallen heroes of 9/11.

team history. Five times he caught more than 100 games as a Met; another year he caught 99. While he notoriously had trouble throwing runners out, he handled pitchers well. No Met ever said he preferred another catcher. (Of course, it helps when you can hit the ball 400 feet.) When a relentless whine turned into a reality and he moved to first base in 2004, people complained because he wasn't Keith Hernandez. He was no Marvelous Marv, either. Piazza didn't want to play there and was annoyed when Art Howe brought it up on TV before talking to him about it. Always the good soldier, he picked up the first baseman's glove and put in a maximum effort.

Piazza rocketed balls to right with the thunder of a left-handed slugger. He hit balls to left like Jimmie Foxx. He crushed pitches against the best pitchers of his era and even took one in the head from the most hotheaded, Roger Clemens. As if the Rocket hadn't done enough, he threw a sawed-off bat in his direction during the 2000 World Series. When he faced Mike Hampton, a newly christened Colorado Rockie who'd complained that Piazza should

TRIVIA

Which Met famously threw a pitch behind, but not at, Roger Clemens on June 15, 2002?

Answers to the trivia questions are on pages 187–189.

have attacked Roger Clemens in the World Series (although Hampton had the ball that night and he could have drilled someone if he so desired), Piazza handled it in his usual manner. He launched a ball off the top of the photographer's box in center field in Hampton's Shea return. When fans talked about what should happen when Piazza faced Clemens at Shea in 2002, Piazza suggested nothing, but he deposited something over the fence against Clemens. Piazza always showed class, even when those around him forgot the meaning of the word.

Bobby Valentine knew the meaning of every word in the dictionary—English as well as Japanese—and he knew every rule in the book. A one-time utility infielder for the Mets, Valentine expertly got under skins in the opposing dugout. Cliff Floyd and David Wells weren't big fans. Felipe Alou managed every game against the Mets like it was Game 7 of the World Series, Tony La Russa bristled at his tactics, and Bobby Cox scowled in his general direction. In his first

TOP 10

Most Influential Mets Coaches

1. **Rube Walker** (1968–1981): Developed the concept of the five-man pitching staff and nurtured the best young talent in franchise history. Tom Seaver and Jerry Koosman thrived under his preaching of patience and mechanics; he helped develop Nolan Ryan into a Hall of Fame Angel/Astro/Ranger. Gil Hodges's right-hand man, Walker also served under Yogi Berra, Roy McMillan, Joe Frazier, and Joe Torre.

2. **Mel Stottlemyre** (1984–1993): Like Rube Walker, Stottlemyre had a stable of great arms to start with, but someone deserved credit for helping raw pitchers Dwight Gooden, Ron Darling, Sid Fernandez, and David Cone become All-Stars. The once and future Yankee lasted more than two decades in a highly criticized position for both local teams in a city of second-guessers.

3. **Yogi Berra** (1965–1971): Even pre-Steinbrenner, the great Yogi was bounced from the Bronx on his ear despite winning a pennant. He came to the Mets as a coach, played a few games, and remained a loyal soldier for more than a decade. He took over as manager following the tragic death of Gil Hodges in 1972.

4. **Bobby Valentine** (1983–1985): While he was still a player, you could see him soaking up the game on the Mets bench in the 1970s. He went to manage in Texas and missed the 1986 celebration. A great teacher, motivator, and speaker often disliked by inferior colleagues.

5. **Bob Apodaca** (1996–1999): Talk about making a lot out of nothing. After arriving with Bobby Valentine late in the '96 season, he turned a staff that couldn't get anyone out into a top-notch group the next year. Rick Reed, anyone? Dack took the axe during a losing streak in '99 because Steve Phillips couldn't fire Bobby V. Dave Wallace did a solid job as his replacement.

6. **Eddie Yost** (1968–1976): Knew the subtleties of the game and judiciously waved his right arm to squeeze as many Mets across home plate as the club's stingy bats could muster. Close your eyes and you can hear Lindsey Nelson say, "And the Walking Man, Eddie Yost, along the lines at third."

7. Rick Peterson (2004–2006): Loses points for coming in under Art Howe and for any influence he might have had in the Scott Kazmir trade. Some scoff at his new-age techniques, but he's had a hand in a resurgence of Tom Glavine, Roberto Hernandez, and Aaron Heilman, among others.

8. Mike Cubbage (1990–1996): A solid minor league manager with the Mets, he should have gotten the New York job instead of Bud Harrelson in 1990 (or better yet, they should've kept Davey Johnson). Cubbage soldiered on, managing the last seven games of 1991, and then serving under Jeff Torborg and Dallas Green. He famously stood up to malcontent mad bomber Vince Coleman.

9. Joe Pignatano (1965–1981): Along with Rube Walker and Eddie Yost, he started with Gil Hodges in Washington. Pignatano and Walker share the longest tenure of any Mets coach. Both followed Joe Torre to Atlanta. Piggy also grew a mean tomato in the Shea bullpen.

10. **Willie Mays** (1974–1979): The most talented Met in uniform during the dismal late 1970s was a coach. Just a glimpse of Willie smiling in the dugout could brighten yet another 7–2 loss to the Phillies. Bowie Kuhn made him quit because he did some work for a casino; now casinos advertise in many parks behind home plate. Say Hey!

Years served as a Mets coach in parentheses.

postseason action, he beat Buck Showalter and managed Cox to a virtual draw (the Braves won on points thanks to Kenny Rogers). The next year he schooled Dusty Baker and La Russa badly as the Mets took the pennant. Joe Torre, his old manager with the Mets, always seemed to have Valentine's number.

Oddly, though, Valentine seemed to do his best work when he didn't have stars. The 1997 club was a patchwork of unwanted parts and he made it hum. Then general manager Steve Phillips loaded up on veterans—pricey ones at that—and went for broke, a high-profile team to go with a back-page manager. Valentine operated the Mets at an excessive speed—probably faster than a club with a rubber-band outfield and aging nucleus could go—and when the club hit a series of bumps in 2002, the driver was thrown from the car.

Valentine spent time as a studio analyst at ESPN, a model of frankness and reliable information that everyone else who holds that role should aspire to. He ran a restaurant in Stamford, Connecticut, where he'd been one of the top high school athletes in the country. Taken with the fifth overall pick by the Dodgers in 1968 (the Mets chose Tim Foli with the first pick in the draft), Valentine shattered his leg and altered his career path climbing a fence in Anaheim in 1973. He apprenticed under Tommy Lasorda, annoying opponents while beating them silly. He coached the Mets, managed the Rangers, became the first American manager in Japan, managed Norfolk, put his heart and soul into the Mets, and finally won a world championship—or as much of a championship as one can win without counting the whole world in the equation—with the Chiba Lotte Marines of Japan. Although you still get the feeling that deep down he'd rather be in the dugout at Shea.

Same goes for Piazza. The son of a well-off car dealer outside Philadelphia, he worked like a dog to make the majors after being drafted as a favor to Lasorda, a family friend. Piazza became a bona fide star under Lasorda in Los Angeles, being voted to the All-Star team and winning Rookie of the Year. He finished in the top 10 in the MVP voting (twice as runner-up) in seven of his first eight seasons. Trading for Piazza was just about the best decision the franchise ever made.

Piazza would have stayed if the Mets had asked, but the sendoff he got from the fans in 2005 made all concerned realize it was best to leave New York on top. Piazza's number 31 waits to be placed on the wall in left field next to Tom Seaver's.

One of the most remarkable things Piazza—or Valentine—ever did occurred in the wake of the devastation of the World Trade Center attacks on September 11, 2001. The Mets had made a 20–5 run and threatened the Braves and second-place Phillies in the NL

That every Met donated a day's salary—approximately $440,000 in all—to Rusty Staub's New York Police and Fire Widows' and Children's Benefit Fund for the game on September 21, 2001?

East, but when the disaster happened, the meaning of the games vanished. With Shea Stadium serving as a staging area, for rescue workers, Valentine packed and unloaded supplies while coordinating help from the Mets. He made appearances, contributed money and food from his restaurant, and worked tirelessly to assist those who needed it. He spent time with the families who'd lost loved ones and he made sure his players realized what their team and their game meant to people in the city and the region.

After 10 days of mourning, baseball returned to New York. Shea Stadium had reverted back into a ballpark and 41,236 came to see the first outdoor sporting event since the attacks. The Mets wore hats to honor the different services that had risked all for the city and their sleeves were embroidered simply, "9–11–01." With the Mets trailing, 2–1, to nemesis Atlanta in the eighth inning, Piazza launched a low fastball from Steve Karsay 420 feet to right-center. After all that had happened, here was a great moment, a baseball moment, that could make people enjoy a game, if only for a few seconds. When the emotion of all that had happened flowed in, it made you want to cry. About everything.

"It is kind of an iconic moment, to say there's a beginning to the healing process, to try to get back to living our lives," Piazza said near the fifth anniversary of the attacks. "As much as everything is etched in memory, all those images, there's a sentiment to move on. Everyone wanted something to cheer about. I'm deeply flattered that people still remember that and put me in that context."

Mets fans will never forget. The Mets may have dropped in the 2001 standings after a pair of agonizing losses to the Braves, but the efforts (both sung and unsung) of Piazza, Valentine, and everyone else in the organization are still among the proudest moments in franchise history. Shea Stadium did its duty. So did its team.

Howe Bad Was It?

Steve Phillips's youth-for-veterans deals seemed inspired when the Mets had talented young players to trade, but it got ugly when the prospects started drying up. He tried trading his problems for other teams' problems, as if an address change would make the player better. Trading Mel Rojas for Bobby Bonilla in 1999, for example, was far worse than simply cutting the ineffective Rojas; the Mets endured the petulant Bonilla's distractions in his second go-round until they worked out deferred payments that would generate income for Bobby Bo into his fifties.

The 2002 deal of Kevin Appier for Mo Vaughn was a similar train wreck. Phillips had erred in giving $10 million a year to the mediocre right-hander in the first place. To get rid of Appier, he took on Mo Vaughn, whose contract was nearly as bloated as the once-feared slugger's frame. He signed Roger Cedeño, Mike Stanton, and David Weathers to multiyear contracts. Even can't-miss deals—Roberto Alomar and then Jeromy Burnitz in exchange for nondescript players—missed horribly. While the four-year deals for Tom Glavine and Cliff Floyd worked out, not to mention the decision to let Edgardo Alfonzo go, Phillips was saved further embarrassment when Japanese star Norihiro Nakamura left the Mets in the lurch and returned home. When Nakamura finally played in the U.S. three years later, he batted .128 as a Dodger.

By August 2002, the Mets were saddled with so much dead weight that they collapsed, going all of August without winning a home game (0–13). Then throw in a 12-game overall losing streak, a six-game losing streak the final week of the season, and not one but two issues regarding players smoking marijuana. Ownership fired

The short-lived Art Howe era is not one that Mets fans embrace today.

Valentine and kept Phillips. The GM had won the five-year battle, but the war was already lost.

Moneyball, the bestseller about Billy Beane's successful Oakland A's, painted Phillips as a cash machine at Beane's disposal, the antithesis of Oakland's smart and thrifty model. Beane, a failed 1980 first-round draft pick of the Mets, had his frustrations, too. His 2002 team lost the Division Series for the third straight year. Author Michael Lewis recreated the Oakland GM's thought process: "The only person in the organization whose riddance would make him happier was his manager, Art Howe," Lewis wrote in *Moneyball.* "It wasn't long before he had a novel idea: trade Art."

The Mets had wanted Lou Piniella, but the Mariners demanded compensation and wouldn't budge from Jose Reyes. The Mets wisely held firm. Piniella was traded to the Devil Rays (for outfielder Randy

Winn), and the Mets got Howe. They would up not even trading anybody for him. You get what you pay for.

In Howe's first season as manager in New York, the Mets were so bad that they...

- Allowed 15 runs on Opening Day, the worst showing ever on day one.
- Endured their most losses in a decade.
- Had their lowest attendance since 1997.
- Were swept in four doubleheaders, all before July, including a two-stadium, day/night debacle against the Yankees.
- Were swept in a season series against the Yankees (0–6), a first since interleague play began in 1997.
- Had a Bentley-driving shortstop, Rey Sanchez, receive a haircut in the clubhouse *during* a blowout loss.
- Were represented at the All-Star Game by their least popular and most disappointing player, Armando Benitez (the alleged clubhouse barber). He was traded to the Yankees the day after the midsummer classic.
- Saw their star catcher's most significant moment turn out to be an inning as a first baseman.
- Had seven non-pitchers hit under .200 (over 20 or more at-bats).
- Had lousy years from, not one, but two Glavines; older brother Tom, and his kid brother Mike, a first baseman who got his only cup of big-league coffee with the lukewarm Mets and hit .143.

IF ONLY . . . Mets management hadn't sided with Steve Phillips over Bobby Valentine at the end of the 2002 season. It was clear that at least one had to go in this adversarial relationship, but while Bobby V. had one bad season out of six— suffered thanks to several questionable players acquired by Phillips—the GM was allowed to remain. He then hired Art Howe. Phillips made a few more dubious moves before he was replaced in June 2003.

By the **NUMBERS** — 5-31—The Mets' September record against wild card or division contenders in 2003 and 2004. So much for Fred Wilpon's mandate of "meaningful games in September." The Mets lost 31 of their first 34 such games under Art Howe until a stunning reversal against Chicago in the penultimate weekend of 2004 sent the Cubs collapsing. Here's how the routs went:

Phillies	0–13
Marlins	1–10
Cubs	2–4
Expos (2003)	2–4

- Led the National League with 506 games started by rookies; three years later only one of them, Jose Reyes, was still with the team.

Jim Duquette was elevated to general manager in midseason—the publication of *Moneyball* and a poor start hadn't helped Phillips—and the former GM's most recent baubles quickly followed: Alomar, Burnitz, Benitez, Sanchez, and Graeme Lloyd. (Royce Ring was the only player acquired in those deals still playing in New York in 2006.) The Mets treaded water for three months without Mike Piazza and used six different first basemen following Vaughn's permanent baseball disability. The year seemed to last forever.

The club went into 2004 spring training with free agent closer Braden Looper; new outfielders Mike Cameron, Shane Spencer, and Karim Garcia; plus a Japanese shortstop, Kaz Matsui, who was said to be so good that the Mets decided to move Jose Reyes to second base. Rookie Tyler Yates fought off several talented youngsters for the last spot in the rotation, and news was spreading about a flame-throwing little lefty, Scott Kazmir, who'd scorched the competition in three different minor leagues...and he was only 20. It had all the makings of a special year. What it ended up being was especially frustrating.

A 14-7 stretch in May catapulted the Mets into contention. The Mets hovered around .500 through most of June and July—they even swept the Yankees at Shea—but as the Mets started to slip in the standings, they made a bold reach. Preposterously bold.

On July 30 they acquired Kris Benson from the Pirates—a deal that had been rumored for weeks—for hard-nosed Ty Wigginton and two prized minor leaguers. The shocker came minutes later when Kazmir, one of the most sought-after young pitchers in baseball, was traded to Tampa Bay for Victor Zambrano, so-so starter with control problems. Fans who'd tried to be patient while the farm system

TRIVIA

The Mets have been the first team to play—and lose—in which two countries?

Answers to the trivia questions are on pages 187–189.

slowly blossomed were livid. The day the Mets made the deal they were three games under .500 and six games out of first place. They never reached .500 again and finished 21 games behind wild-card winner Houston. Howe was fired, Duquette was removed in favor of Omar Minaya, and the Wilpons, who'd bought out Nelson Doubleday two years earlier, receded into the background. It was the club's third-straight losing season. Who knew what the future might hold for the Mets? *New York* magazine, apparently.

An insightful article in *New York* by Alan Schwarz looked at the 2004 Mets and envisioned their lineup in two years. He was right on about the Mets getting Carlos Delgado and Shawn Green, keeping Jose Reyes and Cliff Floyd, a bit off on Kaz Matsui and Jason Phillips, and he didn't see the Kazmir deal coming. No one did. Schwarz nailed the main point, though. "In the playoffs by 2006," he predicted. "Shea Stadium will be rocking again. And the ghost of Roger Cedeño will have been exorcised forever." Amen to that.

"Pedro! Pedro! Pedro!"

Cars had to park in areas of the old World's Fair grounds that hadn't seen life since the Johnson administration (and not Davey Johnson, either). Shea Stadium beer lines lasted two innings or more for those among the 55,351 who dared get up. Fireworks night? No. A playoff game? Nah. It was a day game...in April. And Opening Day had already occurred.

April 16, 2005, marked the Pedro Martinez Met unveiling in New York. He'd already appeared twice on the road. He'd thrown brilliantly on Opening Day in Cincinnati before Braden Looper gave the win away with astonishing speed. Pedro went all the way in his next start, beating John Smoltz's 15-K performance in Atlanta. The Mets had thrown just two complete games in all of 2004, the fewest in franchise history. Pedro would double that himself.

His opponent on that resplendent April Saturday, Al Leiter, had been the club's ace for seven seasons before new general manager Omar Minaya reluctantly decided not to bring him back. There was an outcry in some corners...until the Mets signed Pedro. (See ya, Al.) Leiter and Pedro each allowed three hits through seven innings, but Leiter had a 2–1 lead. Florida's Todd Jones gave it up in the eighth, and Looper let the Marlins tie it in the top of the ninth. Ramon Castro won it for the Mets in the bottom of the ninth, and the Mets, who had started the Willie Randolph regime at 0–5, were now 6–5. Shea was different now. Pedro had arrived.

Pedro first pitched professionally at 16 in the Dominican Summer League in 1988, the same year his brother, Ramon, debuted in Los Angeles. Tommy Lasorda, known for working starters hard, didn't think the slightly built Pedro big enough for him to abuse.

By the NUMBERS

Oldest Current Stadiums by Year Opened

1912	Fenway Park
1914	Wrigley Field
1923	Yankee Stadium
1962	Dodger Stadium
1962	RFK Stadium
1964	**Shea Stadium**
1966	Angel Stadium (original configuration)

After using him as a reliever in 1993, the Dodgers traded Pedro to the Expos for Delino DeShields. Pedro started 117 of 118 games as an Expo and simply became too good for low-budget Montreal to afford. Traded to the Red Sox and remunerated handsomely, he became the best pitcher in the American League, if not baseball. He won three Cy Young Awards (he also placed second twice), and he narrowly missed the 1999 AL MVP. Beyond the hardware, Pedro's status as one of the game's elite made him the perfect target for a team looking to recast its image.

"I told Omar, 'Players don't want to play over here,'" said Tony Bernazard, a former major leaguer and special assistant with the Players Association before becoming Minaya's right-hand man in New York. "There were a number of reasons: bad clubhouse, there was not a tradition of winning, all those things. Pedro was the key to turning that around."

The Mets signed Pedro when the Red Sox, the team he'd just helped win its first World Series since World War I, hesitated at a fourth year. The $53 million allotted for the cornerstone pitcher made other free agents look the Mets' way instead of laugh in their general direction. Carlos Beltran might well have stayed in Houston if they'd offered a no-trade clause, or he may have gone to the Yankees if they'd seemed interested, but he wound up at Shea. Beltran even dubbed the team "the New Mets." While agent Scott Boras actually came up with the catchy name prior to the first meeting with Minaya, it was Beltran who re-christened the franchise

Pedro Martinez's arrival validated the Mets as contenders under Omar Minaya general management and helped forge "the New Mets."

Pitching Performances

1. **Tom Seaver (July 9, 1969)**
   Seaver's perfect game was broken up with one out in the ninth by Jimmy Qualls in front of nearly 60,000 at Shea. With the club contending for the first time and facing the first-place Cubs, Seaver threw the greatest game ever pitched by a Met. In 1975 he would hold the Cubs without a hit until two outs in the ninth (and get a no decision).

2. **Tom Seaver (April 22, 1970)**
   Four days after Nolan Ryan set the club record with 15 Ks, Seaver whiffed 19 Padres, including the last 10 in a row. Jerry Grote said that at one point he stopped giving signs and just held up his glove.

3. **Bobby Jones (October 8, 2000)**
   A Fresno product, like Seaver, Jones pitched a one-hitter to clinch the Division Series against the Giants. He allowed base runners in just one inning in what was his final victory in a Mets uniform.

4. **Al Leiter (October 4, 1999)**
   At the end of perhaps the most stress-filled week in the club's regular-season history, Leiter was magnificent in a one-game playoff in Cincinnati for the wild card. Leiter allowed just two hits to get the Mets in the postseason for the first time in 11 years. Whew!

5. **Dwight Gooden (September 7, 1984)**
   Gooden allowed just one hit against Chicago, which came in the fifth inning when Ray Knight couldn't get Keith Moreland's dribbler out of his glove. Dr. K fanned 11 to set the rookie strikeout record; he'd K 16 in each of his next two starts.

6. **Jerry Koosman (October 16, 1969)**
   Kooz tossed a complete game against the Orioles to clinch the world championship. In his first start of the World Series on October 12, he had taken a no-hitter in the seventh after Seaver had lost Game 1.

7. David Cone (October 6, 1991)
    Overlooked in the mess of the 1991 season, Cone struck
    out 19 Phillies, allowed three hits, and walked one at the
    Vet in the season finale.

8. Pedro Martinez (April 10, 2005)
    Pedro won his first game as a Met after the club's 0–5
    start under rookie manager Willie Randolph, assuring the
    team wouldn't be winless for the home opener. Pedro did
    it in style with a two-hitter to beat John Smoltz at Turner
    Field.

9. Dave Mlicki (June 16, 1997)
    The long rivalry between the Mets and Yankees finally
    spilled out onto the field in the first game ever between the
    two clubs. Dave Mlicki had just two wins until he tossed a
    shutout at Yankee Stadium.

10. Sid Fernandez (October 27, 1986)
    The only relief outing (and incomplete game) on this list is
    by a starter. With Ron Darling knocked out of in the fourth
    inning of Game 7 of the World Series, El Sid came out
    and threw 2⅓ brilliant innings as the Mets rallied for the
    title.

before the media crammed into the Diamond Club for his press conference: "I call it 'the New Mets' because this organization is going to a direction, the right direction—the direction of winning."

Of course, Mets fans would have to see this new direction for themselves. Willie Randolph endured more than a dozen fruitless interviews with other clubs—including one with Mets GM Steve Phillips in 2002—before he became the first African American manager in New York. He showed patience and the ability to adjust on the fly. It didn't hurt that he had Pedro.

Pedro would soak up the spotlight while the Mets scurried around him trying to get everything else in order. He led the National League with a .252 opponent on-base percentage, the best strikeout-to-walk ration (4.43), and the most innings retiring the side in order (93 of 217). His 15–8 record pushed his career winning percentage over .700, the highest in history for any pitcher with 200 decisions. Pedro was 8–2 following a Mets loss and he allowed one run or less

12 times. And for a team without a no-hitter in its history, Pedro twice held opponents hitless long enough to have fans anxiously counting outs. The Astros couldn't get a hit until Chris Burke homered with one out in the seventh inning on June 7. He took it an inning further in Los Angeles on August 14. Antonio Perez tripled to break up the bid in the eighth and then Jayson Werth homered to beat Pedro and end a road trip that featured a devastating outfield collision between Carlos Beltran and Mike Cameron, the worst since Don Hahn and George Theodore collided at Shea in 1973.

Pedro also came up big in areas that are difficult to measure. Notoriously tardy reporting to spring training, Pedro showed up in Port St. Lucie a week early. When a sprinkler went off during a game at Shea, Pedro laughed and danced around where other pitchers would have stormed off the mound or lost their concentration. His driver got lost before his first start at Yankee Stadium as a Met—a game Pedro would rather have skipped—but after an impromptu police escort got him to the ballpark just an hour before game time, Pedro silenced both the Yankees and the "Who's your daddy?" chants that followed him from his Boston days. Pedro had five leads blown by the bullpen, but he did not chastise the struggling relief corps or his manager. He was, in short, a model Pedro.

TRIVIA

Who was the fictional Mets second baseman featured on *Saturday Night Live's* "Weekend Update" in the late 1970s?

Answers to the trivia questions are on pages 187–189.

He was hurting, though. On August 31, the day after Ramon Castro's eighth-inning, three-run home run had put the Mets in a first-place tie with the Phillies for the wild card, Pedro surrendered four home runs to Philadelphia. Pain in his back and right big toe kept him from hitting 90 miles per hour. Yet two start later, after the Mets had spiraled below .500 with six straight losses, Pedro dominated St. Louis and followed that with a shutout of Atlanta as the Mets finished with a 12–4 flourish. It was the complete opposite of the September swoons that had plagued the club every year since 2002. The Mets finished with 83 wins, their highest total since 2000.

It wasn't cause for a ticker-tape parade, but it was progress indeed for these new Mets.

Pedro's physical woes would get worse, however. He gamely gave it a go in 2006 without his best stuff and even won his first five outings, including his 200th career victory. His toe, hip, and torn muscles in both calves kept him from having an impact on 2006; a torn rotator cuff might limit his future. Yet there he was in the dugout the day before his shoulder operation, receiving a standing ovation when he was shown in the dugout during the Division Series (no one could find him during player introductions). Pedro's impact on the Mets remains a mind-and-body experience.

The High Life Again

The Mets had their most dominating club in a generation in 2006. New York rolled over every team in front of them. Only a late Washington rally in the second game of the season kept the Mets from leading the division from wire to wire. Nine wins in their first 10 games catapulted the Mets to the top of the NL East, and they never let another team sniff first place. They finally ended Atlanta's run of division titles at 14. New Mets? You bet.

David Wright became a bona-fide star in 2006, even if his magazine cover–ability sometimes outweighed his productivity. Jose Reyes stopped just short of superstardom, missing the All-Star Game because of a reckless dive into first base and falling just short of team records for runs and steals, plus several other milestones. Still, the free swinger made the naysayers look like fools by collecting the same number of RBIs as strikeouts (81), batting .300, and walking 53 times. And he did it at age 23.

Carlos Delgado, Carlos Beltran, and Wright made the Mets the first New York team to have three players reach 20 home runs at the All-Star break and the first Mets club with three players driving in 114 or more runs. Delgado collected 30 home runs and 100 RBIs for the eighth time in nine seasons. He also joined Gary Carter (1989) and Al Leiter (2000) as Mets who won the Roberto Clemente Award for work in the community.

The big bats benefited Tom Glavine and Steve Trachsel, who won 15 games apiece despite many uneven performances. The Mets used 13 starting pitchers for the year and it could have been more, like picking four random fans to pitch instead of letting Jose Lima go 0–4 with a 9.87 ERA. The bullpen was the best in the NL, and the

Though the postseason end result fell short, Endy Chavez's Game 7 catch reminded a generation of Mets fans of Tommie Agee's and Ron Swoboda's heroics in 1969.

team's overall 4.14 ERA was third in the league. The pitching held up through the postseason; the hitting did not.

The Mets had six regulars bat .300 or better during the Division Series sweep of the Dodgers, but only two starters—Delgado and Shawn Green (each at .304)—did it in the Championship Series loss to the Cardinals. St. Louis held a close edge in every pitching category to earn the pennant and face the Tigers in the World Series. Cliff Floyd, ever the orator in his four years at Shea, spoke after Beltran's bases-loaded strikeout ended Game 7.

"It was the most disappointing thing I've ever been connected with, aside from family issues," said Floyd, who struck out representing the go-ahead run with no outs in the ninth. "To come into this locker room every day has been a joy. To not go to Detroit is a disappointment."

Perhaps younger generations of Mets fans will come to think of Paul Lo Duca's double-tag play at the plate and Endy Chavez's homer-robbing catch with the same reverence as older generations had for the diving plays of Tommie Agee and Ron Swoboda in the 1969 World Series. Of course, those plays had a bigger payoff. In 1969 fans walked up to the window and bought postseason tickets; in 2006, the third three million attendance season in club history, an Internet lottery provided the rare winners with seats deep in the upper deck. The nosebleed seats will be reserved for an even luckier few in the cozier, pricier ballpark (to be christened Citi Field) the Mets began building in 2006.

Will the Mets be better in 2007 and beyond? Turnover at the major league level makes it hard to judge on a yearly basis. Just look at the changes in 2006 compared to '05:

Position　　　　**Who's In, Who's Out**

Catcher　　　　**Paul Lo Duca replaces Mike Piazza**
Just as in L.A., Lo Duca fills in well for Piazza; Paulie hits .318.

First Base　　　　**Carlos Delgado replaces Mike Jacobs**
Jacobs hit four homers in his first four games in the majors, but the second Carlos makes the first Carlos better and the lineup hums.

Second Base   **Jose Valentin replaces Kaz Matsui**
Enough said.

Right Field   **Shawn Green replaces Xavier Nady replaces Mike Cameron**
Cameron is a superior fielder and runner; Nady dominates southpaws; Green's hat flies off frequently.

Reserve Outfielder Endy Chavez replaces Victor Diaz
Endy's finest moments are reminiscent of Melvin Mora in 1999 and 2000.

Pinch Hitter   **Julio Franco replaces Marlon Anderson**
Franco is like having another coach, but lefty-hitting Anderson, 15 years younger (at least), is more useful off the bench.

Pinch Hitter   **Michael Tucker replaces Jose Offerman**
Tucker's not great, but this is a no doubter.

Starting Pitcher   **Orlando Hernandez replaces Jae Seo**
Seo fell off the earth in L.A. and Tampa Bay; if only El Duque's calf had held up in October.

Starting Pitcher   **John Maine replaces Kris Benson**
Maine looks as poised as Benson did as a Pirates rookie.

Starting Pitcher   Oliver Perez replaces Victor Zambrano
Perez is a guy with good stuff who didn't cost Scott Kazmir.

Setup Reliever   **Guillermo Mota replaces Duaner Sanchez replaces Robert Hernandez**
Yes, Hernandez winds up back on the Mets and Mota is an Omar Minaya steal (later suspended for steroid use and re-signed), but if Sanchez had better luck with taxis, the Mets probably would have made the 2006 World Series.

Closer   **Billy Wagner replaces Braden Looper**
To those who whine about Wagner (and every Mets closer since Tug McGraw)—you want Looper back?

Others   **Darren Oliver, Chad Bradford, and Pedro Feliciano**
These pitchers filled areas that the '05 Mets didn't even have capable-enough pitchers for comparison.

TOP 10

Greatest Performances by a Met against the Yankees

1. **Dave Mlicki (June 16, 1997)**
   It all started here. After 35 years of shared existence, interleague play opened Pandora's box. Mlicki hopped out. Entering the game with no career complete games or shutouts, he achieved both in the first real game ever between the two clubs. It's still the best Mets moment in the Bronx. The Mets are 21–32 against the Yankees (regular season) since then.

2. **Matt Franco (July 10, 1999)**
   His two-out, pinch-hit single against Mariano Rivera brought home the tying and winning runs in the bottom of the ninth. It assured the Mets of their first series win against the Yankees.

3. **Ty Wiggington (July 4, 2004)**
   A year after the Mets lost all six games to the Yankees, Wiggy's tiebreaking home run gave the Mets their first weekend Subway sweep and captured a season series against the Yankees for the first time. The false sense of self-worth may have paved the way for some terribly misguided trades, but a sweep is a sweep against the Yankees.

4. **Benny Agbayani (October 24, 2000)**
   The Mets had dropped two games in the Bronx, the Yankees hadn't lost a World Series game in 14 tries, and Orlando Hernandez hadn't lost a postseason game in nine decisions. Benny's hit broke a tie in the eighth. Though doomed to lose the Series, it beat a sweep.

5. **David Wright (May 19, 2006)**
   Great long relief saved the day for the Mets after the Yankees took a big early lead, but Wright was the hero with a tiebreaking double against Mariano Rivera. Hop! Hop!

6. **Mike Piazza (June 9, 2000)**

   Piazza continued his dominance of Roger Clemens with a grand slam in a scoreless game at Yankee Stadium. Clemens showed his true colors by beaning Piazza when they met the next month in the nightcap of a day/night, two-stadium event.

7. **Shawn Estes (June 15, 2002)**

   One of the most overblown incidents in Mets history occurred when Estes couldn't hit Roger Clemens with a pitch to "avenge" Mike Piazza, who'd been beaned and had a shattered bat tossed at him by Clemens in 2000. Estes hit Clemens, all right, with a home run as the Mets ripped the Rocket. Piazza took him deep, too.

8. **Mike Piazza (June 17, 2001)**

   The Mets were mired in a bad stretch and were about to be swept in their first meeting with the Yankees since the World Series, but they rallied for a six-spot in the eighth at Shea on a Sunday night. Tyoshi Shinjo beat out a grounder, and Piazza followed with a two-run homer for the lead.

9. **Luis Lopez (June 28, 1998)**

   Hey, against the '98 Yankees you were lucky to win at all. After the Mets dropped the first two games against the Yankees at Shea, Lopez snapped a tie in the ninth with a long sacrifice fly. Brian McRae almost ruined it with clueless base running in his latter-day impression of Fred Merkle. Umpires be damned, the Mets won.

10. **Casey Stengel (June 20, 1963)**

    Going old school, Casey treated the first Mayor's Trophy Game like it was the World Series. Mets fans did, too. They took over Yankee Stadium and put up banners faster than the Yankees' muscle could tear them down. Casey, who'd done everything he could to win the first spring training game against the Yankees in 1962, did it again in the Bronx in '63. The Mets had an 8–10–1 mark in the New York exhibition.

TRIVIA

Who was the first pitcher to start for both the Yankees and the Mets in the regular-season Subway Series between the New York teams?

Answers to the trivia questions are on pages 187–189.

Meanwhile, the minor leagues yielded talented pitchers Mike Pelfrey, Philip Humber, Brian Bannister, and Alay Soler, all of whom debuted in 2006. Lastings Milledge had his ups and downs and should soon be a major leaguer, somewhere. In one of Minaya's few questionable moves in 2006, Milledge was sent to Norfolk at the end of August and was thus unavailable for the postseason roster. Another speedy outfielder could have helped. That's all water under the Bay now.

All-2000–06 Mets Team

Position	Name
First Baseman	Carlos Delgado
Second Baseman	Jose Valentin
Shortstop	Jose Reyes
Third Baseman	David Wright
Left Fielder	Cliff Floyd
Center Fielder	Carlos Beltran
Right Fielder	Mike Cameron
Catcher	Mike Piazza
Right-handed Pitcher	Pedro Martinez
Left-handed Pitcher	Tom Glavine
Relief Pitcher	Billy Wagner
Overlooked Pitcher	Steve Trachsel
Utility Player	Chris Woodward
Manager	Willie Randolph

That the original Mets announcing crew of Ralph Kiner, Bob Murphy, and Lindsey Nelson worked together longer than any broadcasting trio in baseball history? They started in 1962 and worked together through 1978, when Nelson, the most nationally known of the trio, left to do San Francisco Giants games. Murphy broadcast the Mets through 2003, and Kiner worked several games in 2006. Added together, that's 104 seasons announcing Mets games.

Baseball is a funny game. Despite everything that happened to the pitching staff in October, it really did seem that the 2006 Mets were destined for the World Series until the very last pitch. Each round of playoffs makes it harder to get there (just ask the Yankees), and the increased competition offers no guarantee of success from one year to the next (ask either Sox). For those who live and die orange and blue, the Mets have built toward something special in a very short time. Will it be enough? Watch and see. And dream.

All-Time Team

The Mets have been around since 1962 and have had some great players pass through Shea Stadium. This hypothetical team is based on what happened while a Met, with consideration given for longevity, productivity, and consistency. While hitting has been generally thin with a few notable exceptions, the pitching depth alone over four decades could have filled a 25-man roster. But if the franchise had one game it had to win, this is one man's lineup—Gil Hodges's, presumably—that not many teams would be eager to face.

Starting Lineup

SS	Jose Reyes
2B	Edgardo Alfonzo
1B	Keith Hernandez
C	Mike Piazza
RF	Darryl Strawberry
3B	David Wright
LF	Cleon Jones
CF	Mookie Wilson
P	Tom Seaver

Rotation

LHP	Jerry Koosman
RHP	Dwight Gooden
LHP	Al Leiter
RHP	David Cone

Bullpen
Closer
LHP   Tug McGraw
Setup
LHP   Jesse Orosco
LHP   John Franco
RHP   Roger McDowell
RHP   Armando Benitez
Swingman/Long Man
LHP   Sid Fernandez

Reserves
C   Gary Carter
1B   John Olerud
2B   Ron Hunt
3B   Howard Johnson
OF   Lenny Dykstra
OF   Rusty Staub

Manager
Gil Hodges

Mets Hall of Fame

The Mets inaugurated a Hall of Fame to honor individuals who have meant the most to the team. Plaques honoring these 21 people are on display near the club's World Series trophies in the area next to the Diamond Club at Shea Stadium.

Person	Position	Year Inducted
Joan Payson	Owner	1981
Casey Stengel	Manager	1981
Gil Hodges	Manager	1982
George M. Weiss	President	1982
William A. Shea	Mover and Shaker	1983
Johnny Murphy	General Manager	1983
Lindsey Nelson	Announcer	1984
Bob Murphy	Announcer	1984

Ralph Kiner	Announcer	1984
Bud Harrelson	Shortstop	1986
Rusty Staub	Outfielder	1986
Tom Seaver	Pitcher	1988
Jerry Koosman	Pitcher	1989
Ed Kranepool	First Baseman	1990
Cleon Jones	Outfielder	1991
Jerry Grote	Catcher	1992
Tug McGraw	Pitcher	1993
Mookie Wilson	Outfielder	1996
Keith Hernandez	First Baseman	1997
Tommie Agee	Outfielder	2002
Gary Carter	Catcher	2003

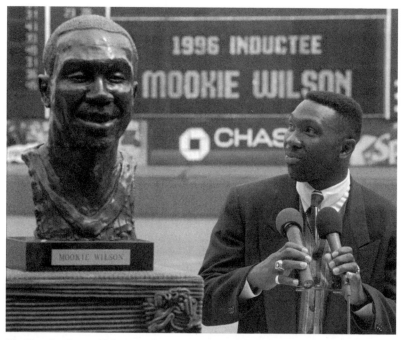

No Mets book would be complete without a photo of Mookie Wilson, the starting center fielder on the all-time Mets team.

ANSWERS TO
TRIVIA QUESTIONS

Page 3: Don Zimmer. Zimmer, not to be confused with a runway model, lived near the Mets' spring training complex in St. Petersburg and thus became the first player photographed wearing the orange and blue.

Page 10: Ron Hunt became the first Met to start in a midsummer classic. He started at second base, representing the Mets in the 1964 All-Star Game, the only one held at Shea Stadium. Hunt singled his first time up and then went hitless the next two at-bats. The game had one of the more thrilling All-Star endings, with the National League rallying in the ninth to tie the game on an error by Yankee Joe Pepitone. After Hank Aaron struck out batting for Hunt, Philadelphia's Johnny Callison won it with a three-run home run.

Page 15: The Mets drafted Les Rohr, who'd win two games in the major leagues, as the second overall pick in the first amateur draft in 1965. The Kansas City A's took Rick Monday with the first-ever selection. Tom Seaver was taken by the Dodgers in the 10th round. Fortunately for the Mets, he went to college instead.

Page 21: It took 14 years, until 1975, before the Mets finally batted higher than .250 as a club. The 1975 Mets, imbued by fine seasons from Felix Millan and Rusty Staub plus newcomers Dave Kingman and Del Unser, batted a robust .256. The 1969 world championship club batted .242 for the season, and the 1973 pennant winners hit .246.

Page 29: Ed Kranepool in 1963, at age 18, was the youngest Met to homer in a game. Kranepool, who debuted with the 1962 club, would hit his last homer in 1979 at age 34, the last original Met in the majors.

Page 35: Jon Matlack and Ron Darling each started three games in a single World Series for the club. Matlack went 1–2 in the 1973 World Series. He dropped the opener, won Game 4, and lost Game 7 to the A's. In 1986 Darling lost his opening start, won his second, and was relieved early in Game 7, before the Mets rallied to beat the Red Sox.

Page 46: Tommie Agee crossed the plate 107 times for the 1970 Mets, becoming the first Met to score more than 100 runs in a season. That year he also became the first Met to have 600 at-bats in a season.

Page 57: With the tying runs on base, Houston's Art Howe flied out to left fielder Dave Kingman, who, like Tom Seaver, was traded three days later. That catch completed Seaver's five-hitter at the Astrodome on June 12, 1977. It was the last win Seaver would earn as a Met until April 20, 1983. Howe would take over the Mets in 2003.

Page 60: The Mets set the record for most singles the same year they established a mark for fewest home runs over a full schedule in 1980. The powerless Mets had 1,087 singles and 61 home runs, the latter resulting in an ongoing *New York Daily News* graphic of whether the 1980 Mets could outhomer Roger Maris's 61 total. The fifth-place Mets tied him.

Page 66: Hubie Brooks. He hit in 24 straight games in 1984, breaking Mike Vail's nine-year-old mark. The night Brooks's streak stopped, fans on Flip-Flop Night paid tribute by littering the field with hundreds of pairs of shower shoes. The Mets never had another shoe promotion, and it took 15 years before Mike Piazza equaled the hitting streak.

Page 73: All six pitchers who had led both leagues in wins, ERA, and strikeouts eventually reached the Hall of Fame: Walter Johnson, Grover Cleveland Alexander, Dazzy Vance, Lefty Grove, Hal Newhouser, and Sandy Koufax. Dwight Gooden broke that mold.

Page 83: Bob Ojeda. The southpaw beat the Astros in a complete game in Game 2 of the NLCS in the Astrodome to even the series. He defeated the Red Sox in Game 3 of the World Series in Boston, where he'd pitched for six seasons before coming to New York, after the Mets had lost the first two games at Shea.

Page 93: Chico Walker made the last out of the division-clincher in 1986. Walker, batting leadoff for Chicago, grounded out to Wally Backman to give the Mets their first division title since 1973. Walker would play for the Mets in 1992 and 1993, homering in his final major league at-bat on October 3, 1993.

Page 95: Danny Heep, batting seventh, singled in two runs as the first designated hitter in Mets history during Game 3 of the 1986 World Series at Fenway Park. Kevin Mitchell also had a hit as a DH in Game 5, and Lee Mazzilli made an out as a pinch hitter in that spot. In all, Mets batters went 2-for-12 in the DH spot. It was another 11 years before regular-season interleague play brought the DH to the NL in road games at AL parks.

Page 107: Rick Aguilera got the win in Game 6 of the 1986 World Series. He allowed the two Boston runs in the top of the tenth that gave Boston its short-lived lead in Game 6. He also hit Bill Buckner with a pitch. Talk about a painful inning for a guy.

Page 114: The Cubs drafted Shawon Dunston, a shortstop with an arm nearly as powerful as Dwight Gooden's, with the first overall pick in 1982. A Brooklyn native and a Mets fan growing up, Dunston played for the Mets in 1999 and was a key man off the bench in the postseason.

Page 123: Lenny Dykstra flied out to center against Mike Bielecki in the top of the first and grounded out against Rich Gossage to end the first completed night game at Wrigley Field in 1988. The Phillies and Cubs had tried it the night before, but the affair was rained out before it was an official game. Under God's own nighttime, the Cubs beat the Mets, 6–4.

Page 127: Gregg Jefferies graced the cover of SI in 1988 after just six at-bats in the big leagues as an '87 call-up. The *Sports Illustrated* cover boy was a three-time MVP in the minors and a two-time *Baseball America* minor league player of the year. His father had famously taught him to swing a bat under water, repeatedly. His explosive September in 1988 was tempered by the anxiety his presence and success caused the veterans. They never warmed to him.

Page 131: Mark Carreon, who played just three full seasons as a Mets bench player and is the son of a former White Sox catcher, hit the most pinch-hit homers (eight) in club history.

Page 137: On a day to honor the reliever for the 300th career save he earned on the previous home stand, John Franco was ejected for his part in an 18-minute brawl. Mets starter Pete Harnisch would be suspended eight games for reaching around the umpire to punch Cubs catcher Scott Servais. Without Franco to protect the lead, Chicago rallied to tie it in the ninth, but Met Rico Brogna won it with a homer.

Page 143: Mike Piazza, Todd Hundley, and Charles Johnson were the three All-Star catchers the Mets briefly had in December 1998. The Mets had Piazza, who'd played in every All-Star Game since 1993 and had just signed a huge contract. Hundley, a two-time All-Star, was sent to the Dodgers for Roger Cedeño and Johnson, who'd caught in the 1997 All-Star Game. Johnson was immediately shipped to Baltimore for Armando Benitez. Say what you will about Cedeño and Benitez in their later New York years, but they were crucial members of the 1999 club.

Page 150: Dennis Cook, who pitched poorly despite a 0.00 ERA in the NLCS, relieved Turk Wendell after Otis Nixon stole second and Brian Jordan had a 2-and-0 count in the seventh inning of Game 5. Cook threw the last two pitches of the intentional walk to Jordan. With the lefty on the mound, Bobby Cox pinch-hit Brian Hunter for dangerous Ryan Klesko. With Cook having fulfilled the requirement of pitching to one batter, and Bobby Valentine having forced Cox's hand, righty Pat Mahomes came in to face Hunter. The Mets got out of the inning and Cook wasn't even charged with a walk.

Page 153: The film *Frequency* incorporated the '69 Mets and the miracle of ham radio for a father and son to connect through time and space, life and death. Dennis Quaid starred with Jim Caviezel, who later played Jesus in Mel Gibson's *The Passion of the Christ*. And some would assert that God likes the Yankees....

Page 159: Shawn Estes started in the big showdown with Roger Clemens in 2002. Many Mets fans screamed for vengeance for Rocket's beaning and bat hurling in Piazza's direction two years earlier. Estes missed Clemens with a pitch, drawing a warning, but he pulled off a squeeze bunt and homered against him, as did Piazza. Estes earned the 8–0 win over the Yankees.

Page 168: The Mets have been the first team to play and lose in both Mexico and Puerto Rico. The Mets were beaten in the first major league game in Mexico by the "host" San Diego Padres, 15–10, in Monterrey on August 16, 1996. The Mets dropped the first game in San Juan to the Montreal Expos by a score of 10–0 on April 11, 2003.

Page 174: Chico Escuela, played by Garrett Morris on *Saturday Night Live*, prospered by his catch phrase: "Baseball...been berry, berry good...to me." Escuela/Morris even traveled to spring training with the Mets in 1979 for a professed comeback. That ended with a Steve Garvey grounder to the crotch. Too bad, the '79 club could've used Chico.

Page 182: Orlando Hernandez made his first start against the Mets in 1998 and appeared against the Yankees in 2006. El Duque's uniform might have changed, but his socks remained just as high.

New York Mets All-Time Roster (through 2006 season)

Players who have appeared in at least one game with the New York Mets.

A

Don Aase (P)	1989
Kurt Abbott (SS)	2000
Juan Acevedo (P)	1997
Benny Agbayani (OF)	1998–2001
Tommie Agee (OF)	1968–72
Rick Aguilera (P)	1985–89
Jack Aker (P)	1974
Manny Alexander (SS)	1997
Edgardo Alfonzo (3B, 2B)	1995–2002
Neil Allen (P)	1979–83
Jermaine Allensworth (OF)	1998–99
Bill Almon (SS)	1980, 1987
Edwin Almonte (P)	2003
Roberto Alomar (2B)	2002–03
Sandy Alomar (2B)	1967
Jesus Alou (OF)	1975
George Altman (OF)	1964
Luis Alvarado (SS)	1977
Craig Anderson (P)	1962–64
Jason Anderson (P)	2003
Marlon Anderson (2B)	2005
Rick Anderson (P)	1986
Bob Apodaca (P)	1973–77
Kevin Appier (P)	2001
Gerry Arrigo (P)	1966
Richie Ashburn (OF)	1962
Tucker Ashford (3B)	1983

Bob Aspromonte (3B)	1971
Pedro Astacio (P)	2002–03
Benny Ayala (OF)	1974–76
Manny Aybar (P)	2005

B

Wally Backman (2B)	1980–88
Mike Bacsik (P)	2002–03
Carlos Baerga (2B)	1996–98
Kevin Baez (SS)	1990, 1992–93
Bob Bailor (OF)	1981–83
Billy Baldwin (OF)	1976
James Baldwin (P)	2004
Rick Baldwin (P)	1975–77
Brian Bannister (P)	2006
Lute Barnes (2B)	1972–73
Jeff Barry (OF)	1995
Kevin Bass (OF)	1992
Ed Bauta (P)	1963–64
Billy Beane (OF)	1984–85
Larry Bearnarth (P)	1963–66
Blaine Beatty (P)	1989–91
Jim Beauchamp (1B)	1972–73
Rich Becker (OF)	1998
Derek Bell (OF)	2000
Gus Bell (OF)	1962
Heath Bell (P)	2004–06
Jay Bell (SS)	2003
Carlos Beltran (OF)	2005–06
Rigo Beltran (P)	1998–99
Armando Benitez (P)	1999–2003

Dennis Bennett (P)	1967	Jerry Buchek (2B)	1967–68
Gary Bennett (C)	2001	Damon Buford (OF)	1995
Kris Benson (P)	2004–05	Tim Burke (P)	1991–92
Butch Benton (C)	1978–80	Jeromy Burnitz (OF)	1993–94, 2002–03
Juan Berenguer (P)	1978–80	Larry Burright (2B)	1963–64
Bruce Berenyi (P)	1984–86	Ray Burris (P)	1979–80
Dwight Bernard (P)	1978–79	Brett Butler (OF)	1995
Yogi Berra (C)	1965	Paul Byrd (P)	1995–96
Jim Bethke (P)	1965		
Steve Bieser (OF)	1997	**C**	
Mike Birkbeck (P)	1992, 1995	Miguel Cairo (2B)	2005
Mike Bishop (C)	1983	Mike Cameron (OF)	2004–05
Willie Blair (P)	1998	Eric Cammack (P)	2000
Terry Blocker (OF)	1985	John Candelaria (P)	1987
Bruce Bochy (C)	1982	John Cangelosi (OF)	1994
Tim Bogar (SS)	1993–97	Chris Cannizzaro (C)	1962–65
Brian Bohanon (P)	1997–98	Buzz Capra (P)	1971–73
Bruce Boisclair (OF)	1974, 1976–79	Jose Cardenal (OF)	1979–80
Dan Boitano (P)	1981	Don Cardwell (P)	1967–70
Mark Bomback (P)	1980	Duke Carmel (OF)	1963
Bobby Bonilla (3B, OF)	1991–95, 1999	Chuck Carr (OF)	1990–91
Mike Bordick (SS)	2000	Mark Carreon (OF)	1987–91
Toby Borland (P)	1997	Gary Carter (C)	1985–89
Don Bosch (OF)	1967–68	Alberto Castillo (C)	1995–98
Daryl Boston (OF)	1990–92	Juan Castillo (P)	1994
Ken Boswell (2B)	1967–74	Tony Castillo (P)	1991
Ricky Bottalico (P)	2004	Ramon Castro (C)	2005–06
Ed Bouchee (1B)	1962	Roger Cedeno (OF)	1998–99, 2002–03
Larry Bowa (SS)	1985	Jaime Cerda (P)	2002–03
Ken Boyer (3B)	1966–67	Rick Cerone (C)	1991
Chad Bradford (P)	2006	Elio Chacon (SS)	1962
Mark Bradley (OF)	1983	Dean Chance (P)	1970
Darren Bragg (OF)	2001	Kelvin Chapman (2B)	1979, 1984–85
Craig Brazell (1B)	2004	Ed Charles (3B)	1967–69
Eddie Bressoud (SS)	1966	Endy Chavez (OF)	2006
Rico Brogna (1B)	1994–96	Bruce Chen (P)	2001–02
Hubie Brooks (3B)	1980–84, 1991	Rich Chiles (OF)	1973
Terry Bross (P)	1991	Harry Chiti (C)	1962
Kevin Brown (P)	1990	John Christensen (OF)	1984–85
Leon Brown (OF)	1976	McKay Christensen (OF)	2002
Mike Bruhert (P)	1978	Joe Christopher (OF)	1962–65
Brian Buchanan (OF)	2004	Galen Cisco (P)	1962–65

Brady Clark (OF)	2002	Jack DiLauro (P)	1969
Mark Clark (P)	1996–97	Steve Dillon (P)	1963–64
Tony Clark (1B)	2003	Jerry Dipoto (P)	1994–96
Donn Clendenon (1B)	1969–71	Chris Donnels (3B)	1991–92
Gene Clines (OF)	1975	Octavio Dotel (P)	1999
Brad Clontz (P)	1998	D.J. Dozier (OF)	1992
Choo Choo Coleman (C)	1962–66	Sammy Drake (2B)	1962
Vince Coleman (OF)	1991–93	Mike Draper (P)	1993
Kevin Collins (3B)	1965, 1967–69	Jeff Duncan (OF)	2003–04
David Cone (P)	1987–92, 2003	Shawon Dunston (OF)	1999
Bill Connors (P)	1967–68	Jim Dwyer (OF)	1976
Cliff Cook (3B)	1962–63	Duffy Dyer (C)	1968–74
Dennis Cook (P)	1997–2001	Lenny Dykstra (OF)	1985–89
Tim Corcoran (1B)	1986		
Mark Corey (P)	2001–02	**E**	
Mardie Cornejo (P)	1978	Tom Edens (P)	1987
Reid Cornelius (P)	1995	Dave Eilers (P)	1965–66
Billy Cowan (OF)	1965	Larry Elliot (OF)	1964–66
Roger Craig (P)	1962–63	Dock Ellis (P)	1979
Jerry Cram (P)	1974–75	Kevin Elster (SS)	1986–92
Joe Crawford (P)	1997	Scott Erickson (P)	2004
Mike Cubbage (3B)	1981	Alex Escobar (OF)	2001
		Nino Espinosa (P)	1974–78
D		Alvaro Espinoza (3B)	1996
Jeff D'Amico (P)	2002	Shawn Estes (P)	2002
Vic Darensbourg (P)	2004	Chuck Estrada (P)	1967
Ron Darling (P)	1983–91	Francisco Estrada (C)	1971
Brian Daubach (1B)	2005	Carl Everett (OF)	1995–97
Ray Daviault (P)	1962		
Kane Davis (P)	2002	**F**	
Tommy Davis (OF)	1967	Jorge Fabregas (C)	1998
Mike DeJean (P)	2004–05	Pete Falcone (P)	1979–82
Carlos Delgado (1B)	2006	Pedro Feliciano (P)	2002–04, 2006
Wilson Delgado (SS)	2004	Sid Fernandez (P)	1984–93
John DeMerit (OF)	1962	Chico Fernandez (SS)	1963
Bill Denehy (P)	1967	Tony Fernandez (SS)	1993
Joe DePastino (C)	2003	Sergio Ferrer (SS)	1978–79
Mark Dewey (P)	1992	Tom Filer (P)	1992
Carlos Diaz (P)	1982–83	Jack Fisher (P)	1964–67
Mario Diaz (SS)	1990	Mike Fitzgerald (C)	1983–84
Victor Diaz (OF)	2004–06	Shaun Fitzmaurice (OF)	1966
Mike DiFelice (C)	2005–06	Don Florence (P)	1995

Gil Flores (OF)	1978–79	Tom Glavine (P)	2003–06
Cliff Floyd (OF)	2003–06	Ed Glynn (P)	1979–80
Doug Flynn (2B)	1977–81	Jesse Gonder (C)	1963–65
Tim Foli (SS)	1970–71, 1978–79	Dicky Gonzalez (P)	2001
Rich Folkers (P)	1970	Geremi Gonzalez (P)	2006
Brook Fordyce (C)	1995	Raul Gonzalez (OF)	2002–03
Bartolome Fortunato (P)	2004, 2006	Dwight Gooden (P)	1984–94
Larry Foss (P)	1962	Greg Goossen (1B)	1965–68
George Foster (OF)	1982–86	Tom Gorman (P)	1982–85
Leo Foster (SS)	1976–77	Jim Gosger (OF)	1969, 1973–74
Joe Foy (3B)	1970	Mauro Gozzo (P)	1993–94
John Franco (P)	1990–01, 2003–04	Bill Graham (P)	1967
Julio Franco (1B)	2006	Wayne Graham (3B)	1964
Matt Franco (1B)	1996–2000	Danny Graves (P)	2005
Jim Fregosi (3B)	1972–73	Dallas Green (P)	1966
Bob Friend (P)	1966	Pumpsie Green (2B)	1963
Danny Frisella (P)	1967–72	Shawn Green (OF)	2006
Mike Fyhrie (P)	1996	Charlie Greene (C)	1996
		Kenny Greer (P)	1993
G		Tom Grieve (OF)	1978
Brent Gaff (P)	1982–84	Jeremy Griffiths (P)	2003
Bob Gallagher (OF)	1975	Jerry Grote (C)	1966–77
Dave Gallagher (OF)	1992–93	Joe Grzenda (P)	1967
Danny Garcia (2B)	2003–04	Lee Guetterman (P)	1992
Karim Garcia (OF)	2004	Eric Gunderson (P)	1994–95
Ron Gardenhire (SS)	1981–85	Mark Guthrie (P)	2002
Jeff Gardner (2B)	1991	Ricky Gutierrez (2B)	2004
Rob Gardner (P)	1965–66		
Wes Gardner (P)	1984–85	**H**	
Wayne Garrett (3B)	1969–76	Don Hahn (OF)	1971–74
Rod Gaspar (OF)	1969–70	Tom Hall (P)	1975–76
Gary Gentry (P)	1969–72	Shane Halter (3B)	1999
John Gibbons (C)	1984, 1986	Darryl Hamilton (OF)	1999–2001
Bob Gibson (P)	1987	Jack Hamilton (P)	1966–67
Paul Gibson (P)	1992–93	Ike Hampton (C)	1974
Shawn Gilbert (2B)	1997–98	Mike Hampton (P)	2000
Brian Giles (2B)	1981–83	Tim Hamulack (P)	2005
Bernard Gilkey (OF)	1996–98	Todd Haney (2B)	1998–99
Joe Ginsberg (C)	1962	Jason Hardtke (2B)	1996–97
Matt Ginter (P)	2004	Shawn Hare (OF)	1994
Mike Glavine (1B)	2003	Tim Harkness (1B)	1963–64

Pete Harnisch (P)	1995–97	Scott Holman (P)	1980–83
Bud Harrelson (SS)	1965–77	Jay Hook (P)	1962–64
Greg Harris (P)	1981	Wayne Housie (OF)	1993
Lenny Harris (OF, 3B)	1998, 2000–01	Mike Howard (OF)	1981–83
Greg Harts (PH)	1973	Pat Howell (OF)	1992
Andy Hassler (P)	1979	John Hudek (P)	1998
Tom Hausman (P)	1978–82	Jesse Hudson (P)	1969
Ed Hearn (C)	1986	Keith Hughes (OF)	1990
Richie Hebner (3B)	1979	Philip Humber (P)	2006
Danny Heep (OF)	1983–86	Todd Hundley (C)	1990–98
Jack Heidemann (SS)	1975–76	Ron Hunt (2B)	1963–66
Aaron Heilman (P)	2003–06	Willard Hunter (P)	1962–64
Bob Heise (SS)	1967–69	Clint Hurdle (C)	1983–85, 1987
Ken Henderson (OF)	1978	Jonathan Hurst (P)	1994
Rickey Henderson (OF)	1999–2000	Butch Huskey (OF)	1993–98
Steve Henderson (OF)	1977–80		
Bob Hendley (P)	1967	**I**	
Phil Hennigan (P)	1973	Jeff Innis (P)	1987–93
Doug Henry (P)	1995–96	Kaz Ishii (P)	2005
Bill Hepler (P)	1966	Jason Isringhausen (P)	1995–97, 1999
Ron Herbel (P)	1970		
Felix Heredia (P)	2005	**J**	
Anderson Hernandez (2B)	2005–06	Al Jackson (P)	1962–65, 1968–69
Keith Hernandez (1B)	1983–89	Darrin Jackson (OF)	1993
Manny Hernandez (P)	1989	Roy Lee Jackson (P)	1977–80
Orlando Hernandez (P)	2006	Mike Jacobs (1B)	2005
Roberto Hernandez (P)	2005–06	Jason Jacome (P)	1994–95
Tom Herr (2B)	1990–91	Gregg Jefferies (1B)	1987–91
Rick Herrscher (1B)	1962	Stan Jefferson (OF)	1986
Orel Hershiser (P)	1999	Chris Jelic (OF)	1990
Jim Hickman (OF)	1962–66	Bob D. Johnson (P)	1969
Joe Hicks (OF)	1963	Bob W. Johnson (SS)	1967
Richard Hidalgo (OF)	2004	Howard Johnson (3B)	1985–93
Joe Hietpas (C)	2004	Lance Johnson (OF)	1996–97
Chuck Hiller (2B)	1965–67	Mark Johnson (1B)	2000–02
Dave Hillman (P)	1962	Barry Jones (P)	1992
Eric Hillman (P)	1992–94	Bobby J. Jones (P)	1993–2000
Brett Hinchliffe (P)	2001	Bobby M. Jones (P)	2000–02
Jerry Hinsley (P)	1964–67	Chris Jones (OF)	1995–96
Gil Hodges (1B)	1962–63	Cleon Jones (OF)	1963–75
Ron Hodges (C)	1973–84	Randy Jones (P)	1981–82

Ross Jones (SS)	1984	Johnny Lewis (OF)	1965–67
Sherman Jones (P)	1962	Dave Liddell (C)	1990
Ricardo Jordan (P)	1997	Cory Lidle (P)	1997
Mike Jorgensen (1B)	1968–71, 1980–83	Jose Lima (P)	2006
Jorge Julio (P)	2006	Jim Lindeman (OF)	1994
		Doug Linton (P)	1993–94
K		Phil Linz (2B)	1967–68
Jeff Kaiser (P)	1993	Mark Little (OF)	2002
Rod Kanehl (2B)	1962–64	Graeme Lloyd (P)	2003
Takashi Kashiwada (P)	1997	Paul Lo Duca (C)	2006
Jeff Kent (2B)	1992–96	Ron Locke (P)	1964
Jeff Keppinger (2B)	2004	Skip Lockwood (P)	1975–79
Dave Kingman (1B, OF)	1975–77, 1981–83	Mickey Lolich (P)	1976
Mike Kinkade (OF)	1998–2000	Phil Lombardi (C)	1989
Wayne Kirby (OF)	1998	Kevin Lomon (P)	1995
Bobby Klaus (2B)	1964–65	Terrence Long (OF)	1999
Jay Kleven (C)	1976	Braden Looper (P)	2004–05
Lou Klimchock (3B)	1966	Luis Lopez (SS)	1997–99
Ray Knight (3B)	1984–86	Al Luplow (OF)	1966–67
Kevin Kobel (P)	1978–80	Ed Lynch (P)	1980–86
Gary Kolb (OF)	1965	Barry Lyons (C)	1986–90
Satoru Komiyama (P)	2002		
Dae-Sung Koo (P)	2005	**M**	
Cal Koonce (P)	1967–70	Rob MacDonald (P)	1996
Jerry Koosman (P)	1967–78	Julio Machado (P)	1989–90
Ed Kranepool (1B)	1962–79	Ken Mackenzie (P)	1962–63
Gary Kroll (P)	1964–65	Elliott Maddox (OF)	1978–80
		Mike Maddux (P)	1993–94
L		Dave Magadan (1B)	1986–92
Clem Labine (P)	1962	Pat Mahomes (P)	1999–2000
Jack Lamabe (P)	1967	John Maine (P)	2006
David Lamb (SS)	2000	Pepe Mangual (OF)	1976–77
Hobie Landrith (C)	1962	Phil Mankowski (3B)	1980, 1982
Ced Landrum (OF)	1993	Jim Mann (P)	2000
Frank Lary (P)	1964–65	Felix Mantilla (2B)	1962
Bill Latham (P)	1985	Barry Manuel (P)	1997
Matt Lawton (OF)	2001	Josias Manzanillo (P)	1993-1995, 1999
Terry Leach (P)	1981–82, 1985–89	Dave Marshall (OF)	1970–72
Tim Leary (P)	1981, 1983–84	Jim Marshall (1B)	1962
Ricky Ledee (OF)	2006	Mike A. Marshall (OF)	1990
Aaron Ledesma (SS)	1995	Mike G. Marshall (P)	1981
Al Leiter (P)	1998–2004	J.C. Martin (C)	1968–69

Jerry Martin (OF)	1984
Tom Martin (P)	2001
Pedro A. Martinez (P)	1996
Pedro J. Martinez (P)	2005–06
Ted Martinez (SS)	1970–74
Roger Mason (P)	1994
Jon Matlack (P)	1971–77
Kazuo Matsui (2B)	2004–06
Gary Matthews (OF)	2002
Mike Matthews (P)	2005
Jerry May (C)	1973
Brent Mayne (C)	1996
Willie Mays (OF)	1972–73
Lee Mazzilli (OF)	1976–81, 1986–89
Jim McAndrew (P)	1968–73
Bob McClure (P)	1988
Rodney McCray (OF)	1992
Terry McDaniel (OF)	1991
Roger McDowell (P)	1985–89
Chuck McElroy (P)	1999
Joe McEwing (OF)	2000–04
Tug McGraw (P)	1965–67, 1969–74
Ryan McGuire (1B)	2000
Jeff McKnight (SS, 2B)	1989, 1992–94
Greg McMichael (P)	1997–99
Roy McMillan (SS)	1964–66
Brian McRae (OF)	1997–99
Kevin McReynolds (OF)	1987–91, 1994
Doc Medich (P)	1977
Carlos Mendoza (OF)	1997
Orlando Mercado (C)	1990
Butch Metzger (P)	1978
Jason Middlebrook (P)	2002–03
Doug Mientkiewicz (1B)	2005
Felix Millan (2B)	1973–77
Lastings Milledge (OF)	2006
Bob G. Miller (P)	1962
Bob L. Miller (P)	1962, 1973–74
Dyar Miller (P)	1980–81
Keith Miller (2B)	1987–91
Larry Miller (P)	1965–66
Ralph Milliard (2B)	1998
Randy Milligan (1B)	1987
John Milner (1B)	1971–77
Blas Minor (P)	1995–96
John Mitchell (P)	1986–89
Kevin Mitchell (OF)	1984, 1986
Vinegar Bend Mizell (P)	1962
Dave Mlicki (P)	1994–98
Herb Moford (P)	1962
Willie Montanez (1B)	1978–79
Joe Moock (3B)	1967
Tommy Moore (P)	1972–73
Bob Moorhead (P)	1962–65
Melvin Mora (OF, SS)	1999–2000
Jerry Morales (OF)	1980
Al Moran (SS)	1963–64
Jose Moreno (OF)	1980
Orber Moreno (P)	2003–04
Kevin Morgan (3B)	1997
Guillermo Mota (P)	2006
Billy Murphy (OF)	1966
Dale Murray (P)	1978–79
Dan Murray (P)	1999
Eddie Murray (1B)	1992–93
Dennis Musgraves (P)	1965
Jeff Musselman (P)	1989–90
Randy Myers (P)	1985–89
Bob Myrick (P)	1976–78

N

Xavier Nady (OF)	2006
Danny Napoleon (OF)	1965–66
Tito Navarro (SS)	1993
Charlie Neal (2B)	1962–63
Randy Niemann (P)	1985–86
C.J. Nitkowski (P)	2001
Junior Noboa (2B)	1992
Joe Nolan (C)	1972
Hideo Nomo (P)	1998
Dan Norman (OF)	1977–80
Edwin Nunez (P)	1988
Jon Nunnally (OF)	2000

O

Charlie O'Brien (C)	1990–93
Tom O'Malley (3B)	1989–90
Alex Ochoa (OF)	1995–97
Jose Offerman (1B)	2005
Bob Ojeda (P)	1986–90
John Olerud (1B)	1997–99
Darren Oliver (P)	2006
Jose Oquendo (SS)	1983–84
Rey Ordonez (SS)	1996–02
Jesse Orosco (P)	1979, 1981–87
Joe Orsulak (OF)	1993–95
Junior Ortiz (C)	1983–84
Brian Ostrosser (SS)	1973
Ricky Otero (OF)	1995
Amos Otis (OF)	1967, 1969
Henry Owens (P)	2006
Rick Ownbey (P)	1982–83

P

John Pacella (P)	1977–80
Tom Paciorek (OF)	1985
Juan Padilla (P)	2005
Craig Paquette (3B)	1998
Harry Parker (P)	1973–75
Rick Parker (OF)	1994
Jose Parra (P)	2004
Tom Parsons (P)	1964–65
Jay Payton (OF)	1998–2002
Bill Pecota (3B)	1992
Al Pedrique (SS)	1987
Mike Pelfrey (P)	2006
Brock Pemberton (1B)	1974–75
Alejandro Pena (P)	1990–91
Oliver Perez (P)	2006
Timo Perez (OF)	2000–03
Yorkis Perez (P)	1997
Robert Person (P)	1995–96
Roberto Petagine (1B)	1996–97
Bobby Pfeil (3B)	1969
Jason Phillips (C)	2001–04
Mike Phillips (SS)	1975–77

Tony Phillips (OF)	1998–99
Mike Piazza (C)	1998–2005
Jim Piersall (OF)	1963
Joe Pignatano (C)	1962
Grover Powell (P)	1963
Todd Pratt (C)	1997–2001
Rich Puig (2B)	1974
Charlie Puleo (P)	1981–82
Bill Pulsipher (P)	1995, 1998, 2000

R

Gary Rajsich (1B)	1982–83
Mario Ramirez (SS)	1980
Len Randle (3B)	1977–78
Willie Randolph (2B)	1992
Bob Rauch (P)	1972
Jeff Reardon (P)	1979–81
Prentice Redman (OF)	2003
Darren Reed (OF)	1990
Rick Reed (P)	1997–2001
Steve Reed (P)	2002
Desi Relaford (SS)	2001
Mike Remlinger (P)	1994–95
Hal Reniff (P)	1967
Jose Reyes (SS)	2003–06
Ronn Reynolds (C)	1982–83, 1985
Tommie Reynolds (OF)	1967
Armando Reynoso (P)	1997–98
Dennis Ribant (P)	1964–66
Gordie Richardson (P)	1965–66
Jerrod Riggan (P)	2000–01
Royce Ring (P)	2005–06
Luis Rivera (SS)	1994
Jason Roach (P)	2003
Kevin Roberson (OF)	1996
Dave Roberts (P)	1981
Grant Roberts (P)	2000–04
Rich Rodriguez (P)	2000
Kenny Rogers (P)	1999
Les Rohr (P)	1967–69
Mel Rojas (P)	1997–98
Jose Rosado (P)	2005

Luis Rosado (1B)	1977, 1980	Don Shaw (P)	1967–68
Don Rose (P)	1971	Norm Sherry (C)	1963
Brian Rose (P)	2001	Tsuyoshi Shinjo (OF)	2001, 2003
Don Rowe (P)	1963	Craig Shipley (SS)	1989
Glendon Rusch (P)	1999–2001	Bart Shirley (2B)	1967
Dick Rusteck (P)	1966	Bill Short (P)	1968
Nolan Ryan (P)	1968–71	Paul Siebert (P)	1977–78
		Doug Simons (P)	1991
S		Ken Singleton (OF)	1970–71
Bret Saberhagen (P)	1992–95	Doug Sisk (P)	1982–87
Ray Sadecki (P)	1970–74, 1977	Bobby Gene Smith (OF)	1962
Joe Sambito (P)	1985	Charley Smith (3B)	1964–65
Amado Samuel (SS)	1964	Dick Smith (OF)	1963–64
Juan Samuel (OF)	1989	Pete Smith (P)	1994
Duaner Sanchez (P)	2006	Esix Snead (OF)	2002, 2004
Rey Sanchez (SS)	2003	Duke Snider (OF)	1963
Ken Sanders	1975–76	Alay Soler (P)	2006
Rafael Santana (SS)	1984–87	Warren Spahn (P)	1965
Jose Santiago (P)	2005	Tim Spehr (C)	1998
Mackey Sasser (C)	1988–92	Shane Spencer (OF)	2004
Doug Saunders (2B)	1993	Bill Spiers (3B)	1995
Rich Sauveur (P)	1991	Dennis Springer (P)	2000
Mac Scarce (P)	1975	Steve Springer (3B)	1992
Jimmie Schaffer (C)	1965	Larry Stahl (OF)	1967–68
Dan Schatzeder (P)	1990	Roy Staiger (3B)	1975–77
Calvin Schiraldi (P)	1984–85	Tracy Stallard (P)	1963–64
Al Schmelz (P)	1967	Leroy Stanton (OF)	1970–71
Dave Schneck (OF)	1972–74	Mike Stanton (P)	2003–04
Dick Schofield (SS)	1992	Rusty Staub (OF)	1972–75, 1981–85
Pete Schourek (P)	1991–93	John Stearns (C)	1975–84
Ted Schreiber (3B)	1963	John Stephenson (C)	1964–66
Don Schulze (P)	1987	Randy Sterling (P)	1974
Mike Scott (P)	1979–82	Kelly Stinnett (C)	1994–95, 2006
Marco Scutaro (2B)	2002–03	George Stone (P)	1973–75
Ray Searage (P)	1981	Pat Strange (P)	2002–03
Tom Seaver (P)	1967–77, 1983	Darryl Strawberry (OF)	1983–90
David Segui (1B)	1994–95	Scott Strickland (P)	2002–03
Dick Selma (P)	1965–68	John Strohmayer (P)	1973–74
Frank Seminara (P)	1994	Brent Strom (P)	1972
Jae Seo (P)	2002–05	Dick Stuart (1B)	1966
Art Shamsky (OF)	1968–71	Tom Sturdivant (P)	1964
Bob Shaw (P)	1966–67	Bill Sudakis (3B)	1972

John Sullivan (C)	1967	Bubba Trammell (OF)	2000
Darrell Sutherland (P)	1964–66	Alex Trevino (C)	1978–81, 1990
Craig Swan (P)	1973–84	Ricky Trlicek (P)	1996
Rick Sweet (C)	1982	Michael Tucker (OF)	2006
Ron Swoboda (OF)	1965–70	Wayne Twitchell (P)	1979
		Jason Tyner (OF)	2000

T

Pat Tabler (OF)	1990	**U**	
Shingo Takatsu (P)	2005	Del Unser (OF)	1975–76
Jeff Tam (P)	1998–99		
Frank Tanana (P)	1993	**V**	
Kevin Tapani (P)	1989	Mike Vail (OF)	1975–77
Tony Tarasco (OF)	2002	Eric Valent (OF)	2004–05
Randy Tate (P)	1975	John Valentin (3B)	2002
Jim Tatum (1B)	1998	Jose Valentin (2B)	2006
Frank Taveras (SS)	1979–81	Bobby Valentine (2B)	1977–78
Billy Taylor (P)	1999	Ellis Valentine (OF)	1981–82
Chuck Taylor (P)	1972	Julio Valera (P)	1990–91
Hawk Taylor (C)	1964–67	Mo Vaughn (1B)	2002–03
Ron Taylor (P)	1967–71	Jorge Velandia (SS)	2000–01, 2003
Sammy Taylor (C)	1962–63	Robin Ventura (3B)	1999–2001
Dave Telgheder (P)	1993–95	Tom Veryzer (2B)	1982
Garry Templeton (SS)	1991	Fernando Vina (2B)	1994
Walt Terrell (P)	1982–84	Frank Viola (P)	1989–91
Ralph Terry (P)	1966–67	Joe Vitko (P)	1992
Tim Teufel (2B)	1986–91	Jose Vizcaino (SS)	1994–96
George Theodore (OF)	1973–74		
Frank Thomas (OF)	1962–64	**W**	
Ryan Thompson (OF)	1992–95	Billy Wagner (P)	2006
John Thomson (P)	2002	Bill Wakefield (P)	1964
Lou Thornton (OF)	1989–90	Chico Walker (3B)	1992–93
Marv Throneberry (1B)	1962–63	Pete Walker (P)	1995, 2001–02
Gary Thurman (OF)	1997	Tyler Walker (P)	2002
Dick Tidrow (P)	1984	Donne Wall (P)	2001
Rusty Tillman (OF)	1982	Derek Wallace (P)	1996
Jorge Toca (1B)	1999–2001	Gene Walter (P)	1987–88
Jackson Todd (P)	1977	Claudell Washington (OF)	1980
Andy Tomberlin (OF)	1996–97	Allen Watson (P)	1999
Joe Torre (1B)	1975–77	Matt Watson (OF)	2003
Mike Torrez (P)	1983–84	David Weathers (P)	2002–04
Kelvin Torve (1B)	1990–91	Hank Webb (P)	1972–76
Steve Trachsel (P)	2001–06	Al Weis (2B)	1968–71

Turk Wendell (P)	1997–2001	Herm Winningham (OF)	1984
David West (P)	1988–89	Gene Woodling (OF)	1962
Mickey Weston (P)	1993	Chris Woodward (2B)	2005–06
Dan Wheeler (P)	2003–04	David Wright (3B)	2004–06
Rick White (P)	2000–01	Billy Wynne (P)	1967
Wally Whitehurst (P)	1989–92		
Ty Wigginton (3B)	2002–04	**Y**	
Rick Wilkins (C)	1998	Tyler Yates (P)	2004
Carl Willey (P)	1963–65	Masato Yoshii (P)	1998–99
Nick Willhite (P)	1967	Anthony Young (P)	1991–93
Charlie Williams (P)	1971	Joel Youngblood (OF)	1977–82
Dave Williams (P)	2006		
Gerald Williams (OF)	2004–05	**Z**	
Paul Wilson (P)	1996	Pat Zachry (P)	1977–82
Mookie Wilson (OF)	1980–89	Victor Zambrano (P)	2004–06
Preston Wilson (OF)	1998	Todd Zeile (1B)	2000–01,
Tom Wilson (C)	2004		2004
Vance Wilson (C)	1999–2004	Don Zimmer (3B)	1962

Notes

The Mahatma and the Conjuring of the Mets
"In my coat pocket. Where else?" Pietrusza, David, *Major Leagues*, Jefferson, North Carolina: McFarland & Company, 1991.

Casey Calls the Tune
"Forget it Casey, he missed second, too." Pietrusza, David, Matthew Silverman, and Michael Gershman, *Baseball: The Biographical Encyclopedia*, Kingston, New York: Total Sports Illustrated, 2000.
"...a real cliff dweller" and "Baseball is like church..." Pietrusza, David, Matthew Silverman, and Michael Gershman, *Baseball: The Biographical Encyclopedia*, Kingston, New York: Total Sports Illustrated, 2000.

Stumbling on the Franchise
"There was an aura of defeatism and I refused to accept it..." Bock, Duncan and John Jordan, *The Complete Year-by-Year N.Y. Mets Fan's Almanac*, Balliet & Fitzgerald, New York: Crown Publishers, 1992.

The Greatest: Gil Hodges
"When he was young and immature and nervous, he used to jump up and down..." Bock, Duncan and John Jordan, *The Complete Year-by-Year N.Y. Mets Fan's Almanac*, Balliet & Fitzgerald, New York: Crown Publishers, 1992.
"...unfair, unreasonable, unfeeling, incapable of handling men, stubborn, holier-than-thou and ice-cold." "The Little Team That Can," *Time*, September 5, 1969.

METS ESSENTIAL

"Hodges is one hell of a leader..." "The Little Team That Can," *Time*, September 5, 1969.

"My main goal was to change the notion that everything the Mets did was wrong..." "The Little Team That Can," *Time*, September 5, 1969.

Kooz

"I figured I'd better sign before I owed them money." Baseball-almanac.com.

Screwball Tug

"...the confidence I would ride the rest of my career." McGraw, Tug and Joseph Durso, *Screwball*, Boston: Houghton Mifflin Company, 1974.

"It took 20 minutes to say what should have taken five." McGraw, Tug and Don Yaeger, *Ya Gotta Believe*, New York: New American Library, 2004.

"...about the size of a poached egg..." McGraw, Tug and Don Yaeger, *Ya Gotta Believe*, New York: New American Library, 2004.

"Ten million years from now, when the sun burns out and the earth is just a frozen iceball..." baseball-reference.com.

Yogi Gotta Believe

"Top 10." Berra, Yogi, *The Yogi Book*, New York: Workman Publishing, 1998.

Number 8 in Top 10: "You give us Jonesy and Rusty and Milner playing a full season..." Bock, Duncan and John Jordan, *The Complete Year-by-Year N.Y. Mets Fan's Almanac*, Balliet & Fitzgerald, New York: Crown Publishers, 1992.

Bad Moves Risin'

"We've had him three full years and, although he's a hell of a prospect, he hasn't done it for us . . . ." Joseph Durso, "Mets Trade Ryan," *The New York Times*, December 10, 1971.

"...the best arm in the National League and at 24, he's just coming into his own." Joseph Durso, "Mets Trade Ryan," *The New York Times*, December 10, 1971.

"He could put things together overnight." Joseph Durso, "Mets Trade Ryan," *The New York Times*, December 10, 1971.

"No one knew the organization better than Whitey...." ("If Only"). Lang, Jack, and Peter Simon, *The New York Mets: Twenty-Five Years of Baseball Magic*, New York: Henry Holt and Company, 1986.

Grant's Tomb

"Nolan Ryan is getting more money than Tom Seaver and that galls Tom . . ." Bock, Duncan and John Jordan, *The Complete Year-by-Year N.Y. Mets Fan's Almanac*, Balliet & Fitzgerald, New York: Crown Publishers, 1992.

"I hate to think how lousy they're going to be in a couple of years." Bock, Duncan and John Jordan, *The Complete Year-by-Year N.Y. Mets Fan's Almanac*, Balliet & Fitzgerald, New York: Crown Publishers, 1992.

Coming Soon: Hope

"What the heck, Frank is an old friend . . ." Lang, Jack, and Peter Simon, *The New York Mets: Twenty-Five Years of Baseball Magic*, New York: Henry Holt and Company, 1986.

"And pitching number 41 . . ." Lang, Jack, and Peter Simon, *The New York Mets: Twenty-Five Years of Baseball Magic*, New York: Henry Holt and Company, 1986.

Managing a Turnaround

"The New York Mets were in absolute shambles when I took over as manager in October 1983..." Johnson, Davey and Peter Golenbock, *Bats*, New York: Putnam, 1986.

"My plan at the start of the season was for four of the five pitchers in my rotation to be young..." Johnson, Davey and Peter Golenbock, *Bats*, New York: Putnam, 1986.

"After seeing him in those two games I made up my mind..." Lang, Jack, and Peter Simon, *The New York Mets: Twenty-Five Years of Baseball Magic*, New York: Henry Holt and Company, 1986.

Unlucky at Cards

"He made it up." Johnson, Davey and Peter Golenbock, *Bats*. New York: Putnam, 1986.

"The bench was rolling, Hernandez hid his face in his glove..." Bock, Duncan and John Jordan, *The Complete Year-by-Year N.Y. Mets Fan's Almanac*, Balliet & Fitzgerald, New York: Crown Publishers, 1992.

"We've come this far..." Johnson, Davey and Peter Golenbock, *Bats*, New York: Putnam, 1986.

"How could I know what the percentage was? ..." Hernandez, Keith and Mark Bryan, *If at First*, New York: McGraw-Hill Book Company, 1986.

"...would push one of my four young starters, Aguilera or Fernandez..." ("Did You Know"). Johnson, Davey and Peter Golenbock, *Bats*, New York: Putnam, 1986.

Mex: The Met You'd Want in Your Foxhole

"Playing near family is tough..." Hernandez, Keith and Mark Bryan, *If at First*, New York: McGraw-Hill Book Company, 1986.

"The Siberia of baseball." Hernandez, Keith and Mark Bryan, *If at First*, New York: McGraw-Hill Book Company, 1986.

"I decided the Mets had a chance to be a better ballclub in 1984..." Hernandez, Keith and Mark Bryan, *If at First*, New York: McGraw-Hill Book Company, 1986.

"They're great fans..." George Vescey, "'Only Barometer' for Hernandez," *The New York Times*, September 11, 1985.

"As Keith goes, the team goes." Johnson, Davey and Peter Golenbock, *Bats*, New York: Putnam, 1986.

"If I can hit .300 with all the things I've been through this year..." Johnson, Davey and Peter Golenbock, *Bats*, New York: Putnam, 1986.

"He can't handle your breaking ball. Forget the fastball..." Marty Noble, "Orosco to Throw Out First Pitch to Carter," MLB.com, March 20, 2006.

"By the Numbers: 17." Jon Springer, MBTN.net.

One Oh Eight, Eighty-Six
"I could see the frustration in their faces…" Bock, Duncan and John Jordan, *The Complete Year-by-Year N.Y. Mets Fan's Almanac*, Balliet & Fitzgerald, New York: Crown Publishers, 1992.

"And a Ground Ball Trickling…"
"If [Scott] doesn't scuff it up…" Ron Darling. "It's Tough Scuff Stuff." *New York Daily News*, October 14, 1986.

"His status for the World Series is questionable." Listed under "Baseball Almanac," *New York Daily News*, October 17, 1986.

"To me that was the turning point." Pearlman, Jeff. *The Bad Guys Won!* New York: HarperCollins, 2004.

"Being down 2–0 and not checking out our ballpark…" Pearlman, Jeff. *The Bad Guys Won!* New York: HarperCollins, 2004.

"And a Ground Ball Trickling…" MLB.com.

Messy Jesse
"Who's Orosco?" Lang, Jack, and Peter Simon, *The New York Mets: Twenty-Five Years of Baseball Magic*, New York: Henry Holt and Company, 1986.

"I have to be careful how I use him." Lang, Jack, and Peter Simon, *The New York Mets: Twenty-Five Years of Baseball Magic*, New York: Henry Holt and Company, 1986.

"You have the ball . . ." Jim Naughton, "A Profile in Courage," *New York Daily News*, October 16, 1986.

"The World Series … can only be an anti-climax." Phil Pepe, "Marathoners for Mets Win Race to Flag," *New York Daily News*, October 16, 1986.

A Championship Hangover
"…letting his teammates down." Bock, Duncan and John Jordan, *The Complete Year-by-Year N.Y. Mets Fan's Almanac*, Balliet & Fitzgerald, New York: Crown Publishers, 1992.

"Nobody I know gets sick 25 times a year." Bock, Duncan and John Jordan, *The Complete Year-by-Year N.Y. Mets Fan's Almanac*, Balliet & Fitzgerald, Inc., New York: Crown Publishers, 1992.

"Little redneck." Bock, Duncan and John Jordan, *The Complete Year-by-Year N.Y. Mets Fan's Almanac*, Balliet & Fitzgerald, Inc., New York: Crown Publishers, 1992.

"Going to Smithers was a cover-up..." Sokolove, Michael, *The Ticket Out*, New York: Simon & Schuster, 2004.

"When he wanted to be, he was as good as it gets..." Sokolove, Michael. *The Ticket Out*, New York: Simon & Schuster, 2004.

"In 1985, Dwight Gooden was a real life Sidd Finch." McCarver, Tim and Ray Robinson, *Oh, Baby, I Love It!* New York: Villard Books, 1987.

"Dwight Gooden and Darryl Strawberry were the guys who really let us down," Pearlman, Jeff. *The Bad Guys Won!* New York: HarperCollins, 2004.

Where's Randy?

"Lucky" and "high school pitcher." Bock, Duncan and John Jordan, *The Complete Year-by-Year N.Y. Mets Fan's Almanac*, Balliet & Fitzgerald, Inc., New York: Crown Publishers, 1992.

A Distant Second

"We don't deserve to win." Bock, Duncan and John Jordan, *The Complete Year-by-Year N.Y. Mets Fan's Almanac*, Balliet & Fitzgerald, Inc., New York: Crown Publishers, 1992.

"Simply put, we don't win two pennants without him." Al Doyle, "Bud Harrelson: The Game I'll Never Forget," *Baseball Digest*, August 2005.

"What no one could have known was how insecure and paranoid he would be..." Klapisch, Bob and John Harper, *The Worst Team Money Could Buy*, New York: Random House, 1993.

Money for Nothing

"I know what you all are gonna try, but you're not gonna wipe this smile off my face..." Klapisch, Bob and John Harper, *The Worst Team Money Could Buy*. New York: Random House, 1993.

Crawling from the Wreckage
"People thought we were the second coming up in New York..." Seth
 Livingstone. "Generation K: Sidetracked from Stardom." *USA
 TODAY Sports Weekly*, June 30–July 5, 2004.

The Winning Team
"On the left side of the infield Ventura and Ordonez..." Tom
 Verducci, "Glove Affair," *Sports Illustrated*, September 16, 1999.
"What's really impressive is that they don't even play on a great field
 at Shea..." Tom Verducci, "Glove Affair," *Sports Illustrated*,
 September 16, 1999.

Leiter, Pratt, and the Grand-Slam Single
"It should have been an easy catch..." Blatt, Howard, *Amazin' Met
 Memories*, Tampa: Albion Press, 2002.
"I wanted to cry." Blatt, Howard, *Amazin' Met Memories*, Tampa:
 Albion Press, 2002.
"Two celebrations in one week after waiting my whole career for
 one." Blatt, Howard. *Amazin' Met Memories*. Tampa: Albion
 Press, 2002.

Building on Success
"This was the one thing we lacked..." Jayson Stark. "Hampton's
 Glorious Game Gets Mets to Series." ESPN.com, October 18,
 2000.

Mikey P. and Bobby V.
"You're not dealing with real professionals in the clubhouse..."
 Golenbock, Peter. *Amazin'*, New York: St. Martin's, 2002.
"Bobby makes things easier for the players..." Golenbock, Peter.
 Amazin', New York: St. Martin's, 2002.
"It is kind of an iconic moment..." Lyle Spencer, MLB.com,
 September 8, 2006.

Howe Bad Was It?
"The only person in the organization whose riddance would make
    him happier..." Lewis, Michael, *Moneyball*, New York, W.W.
    Norton & Co., 2003.
"In the playoffs in 2006..." Alan Schwarz, "Re-engineering the Mets,"
    New York, May 3, 2004.

"Pedro! Pedro! Pedro!"
"I told Omar, 'Players don't want to play over here...' " Ray Sánchez,
    "Hispanic Players Help Mets Win Big," *Newsday*, October 22,
    2006.
"I call it 'the New Mets' because this organization is going to a direc-
    tion..." Rubin, Adam, *Pedro, Carlos, and Omar*, Guilford,
    Connecticut: The Lyons Press, 2006.

The High Life Again
"It was the most disappointing thing I've ever been connected
    with..." David Lennon, "For Mets It's a World of Pain," *Newsday*,
    October 20, 2006.